Barra and Skye:
Two Hebridean Perspectives

Barra and Skye:
Two Hebridean Perspectives

Arne Kruse
Editor

Alasdair Ross
Assistant Editor

The Scottish Society for Northern Studies
Edinburgh 2006

Published in Scotland by
The Scottish Society for Northern Studies
c/o Celtic and Scottish Studies
School of Literatures, Languages and Cultures
University of Edinburgh
27 George Square
Edinburgh EH8 9LD

ISBN 0-9535226-3-6

Cover photographs – front: Vatersay, Barra – back: Skye – by Brigitte Guénier.

Printed by Shetland Litho,
Gremista, Lerwick, Shetland ZE1 0PX

Contents

Foreword

THE volume you are now holding contains a selection of papers given at two separate conferences arranged by the Scottish Society for Northern Studies. The first conference took place in Castlebay, Barra, in April 2002, and the second conference was arranged at Sabhal Mór Ostaig, Teangue on the Isle of Skye in April 2003.

These nine papers, five about aspects of Barra and four concerning Skye, are not meant to offer anything like a consolidated line of history of the two islands. They do, however, bring together facets of research from highly respected authorities within their own specialities, concerning the islands' past and present times. The compilation of articles reflects the very multi-disciplinary approach taken by the Scottish Society for Northern Studies.

This book would of course never have happened were it not for the Scottish Society for Northern Studies and the Society's programme of annual conferences in Scotland and beyond. Over the years this series of conferences has brought together local historians and academic experts and has activated interest and pride in many aspects of the history of regions and local communities. A string of publications has resulted from many of the conferences, of which the current volume is one.

The spelling of place-names in the articles is mostly left to the individual authors but most have followed the principle that since this volume is in the English language English spelling will be used when there is an established tradition for it. In practice this means that Gaelic spelling is used for smaller places and English for larger locations like towns and islands.

Some people have contributed substantially to this book, and both their support and practical help need to be acknowledged. Alasdair Ross was in charge of the Skye section until the final stages of the editing process and has, in practice, functioned as a co-editor of the book. In addition to having written one of the articles, Ian R. Macneil of Barra has helped out with the process of turning Calum MacNeil's talk into a readable format. He arranged for the recording of the talk, aided with the editing and proofreading of the text and, finally, he has written a useful comment on Calum's contribution. The Macneil's knowledge of the history and people of Barra is extremely valuable, and he has shared it generously. Anke Beate Stahl also contributed with an article in addition to having transcribed Calum MacNeil's talk. These three, more than any others, have helped to bring this book into existence. We believe that it makes a significant contribution towards a better understanding of an exciting part of the world.

Arne Kruse
December 2005
Edinburgh

Barra

Barra – the Physical Background

Noel Fojut

AS WITH all islands, the physical facts of Barra's location, geology and climate have a profound influence upon the nature of life for inhabitants and visitors. Even today the constraints of time, tide and weather are no respecters of timetables, while weather variations within a single day can give the lie to the changing seasons. How much more so in, centuries past, must the physical geography of Barra have determined human options, closing off opportunities with one hand while opening up connections with the other. Determinism may be an unpopular concept in modern science, yet anyone spending a winter on Barra might think again.

Barra's story begins in an unimaginably distant geological past. An area of lighter crustal rocks, a 'craton' as geologists of 3000 million years later would term it, formed the basis for an early continent (Fettes *et al* 1992: *passim*)[1]. This area, of unknown extent but including much of what is today the Western Isles, rode high above the heavier rocks of the ocean floor. Despite endless crustal movements, continents spreading and being destroyed, oceans opening and closing, these rocks remained unabsorbed. Most of the upper crust of the Earth from that early date has long been re-cycled, drawn down into the lower reaches, melted and re-cycled. But not the rocks of Barra. Despite intense pressure and folding, sometimes as much as 25 km below the surface at the root of an ancient mountain chain comparable to the Alps or the Andes, they survived, to form what today we call the Lewisian gneiss.

The gneiss, with its distinctive grey hues mottled with patches of granite, was already ancient when crustal movements created a huge fault. Running the full length of the east coast of the Long Island, this is the Outer Hebrides Thrust,

---

1   Fettes *et al* 1992 covers the Outer Hebrides. It is intensely detailed, requiring good geological knowledge to read with any degree of profit. Boyd and Boyd 1996:11-29 provides a good non-technical geological summary for the whole of the Hebrides.

created around 1700 million years ago. Rocks from the east rode up westwards over more recent rocks, in a manner analogous to the better-known Moine Thrust of the North West Highlands. Recent research has suggested that at times the Thrust later acted as a normal fault, with younger rocks displaced downwards to the east, towards the Minch. Research work continues – a fault line so ancient will have had more than one incarnation, and with movements in both normal and reversed directions during its long life. There are still occasional movements along the fault today.

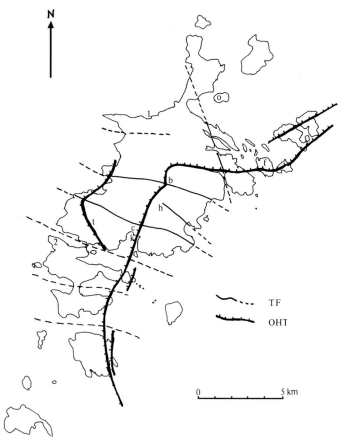

Fig 1 Geological features affecting the modern landscape of Barra: OHT = Outer Hebrides Thrust; TF = tension faults. Key locations mentioned in text: b = Beul a'Bhealaich; c = Castlebay; f = Fuiay; h = Heaval; k = Kisimul Castle; o = Orosay; t = Ben Tangaval; 1 = Cleat; 2 = Traigh Varlish.

The Outer Hebrides Thrust, which like most thrusts is composed of several sub-parallel lines of movement, is clearly visible in the landscape of present-day Barra. Crushing and sliding movements along a broad plane transformed the rocks on each side of the fault, creating harder rocks where heat was generated by the movements and softer rocks where crushing was predominant. The large slab of rocks running uphill behind Castlebay toward the summit of Heaval is composed of rocks partially liquidised and reset. Kisimul Castle sits directly on the fault, its rock made a little harder than the surroundings. The gaps between the rocky islands at the northeast end of Vatersay, so clearly visible from Castlebay, correspond to rocks crushed by fault movements. A band of altered rock along the fault line runs very visibly across Fuiay, off the eastern entrance to Northbay. On the west side of Barra a secondary fault, apparently of the same age, curves around the west side of Ben Tangaval.

Then, for a little over a mere 1000 million years, there is no record of geological change: for most of this time, no doubt, modern Barra lay deep below crumbling mountains, slowly rising as erosion removed the vast overburden, which was washed off in great sheets of sands and gravels, some of which went to form the Torridonian sedimentary rocks of the western seaboard of the Scottish mainland.

About 400 million years ago, crustal movements reawakened the old continental core of the Outer Hebrides once more. The great fault was reactivated, and as mountains built up over what was to become the Scottish mainland the crust was stretched slightly, creating a series of faults that now run more or less east to west across Barra. These became lines of weakness to be exploited by later erosion, and today are dominant landscape features. The gaps between Barra and Vatersay, the dip running from Borve up the valley and under Beul a Bhealaich across to Earsary and, running north-west to south-east, the fault which runs across the inner end of Ardmhor and forms the seaward portion of Loch Obe, are all examples of Caledonian fault lines. Meanwhile the Minch, formed by down-faulting along a north-south line running offshore just to the east of the Outer Hebrides Thrust, had become what it remains today – a great fault-defined trough into which sediments were washed from surrounding shores.

Over the millennia, Barra may have been submerged from time to time, receiving a capping of sedimentary rocks, but any such deposits have long since eroded. The general pattern, of the Outer Hebrides riding high on the western edge of an active geological zone, continued until relatively recent times. 70 million years ago the Atlantic began to open, accompanied by a great burst of volcanic activity, which threw up the great gabbro masses of the Rum and Skye Cuillin and the complex rocks of Mull and Ardnamurchan. The opening of the Atlantic split Greenland and Labrador apart from Western Scotland. The landscapes of most of the Inner Hebrides were dramatically transformed at this time, with the creation of distinctive volcanic features, especially in Skye, Mull and Rum. But on Barra, only a few dykes of intruded igneous rock mark the violence experienced a few kilometres to the east. Examples may be seen along the northwest shore of Vatersay, around Traigh Varlish, and on the headland leading towards Orosay at Eoligarry. These dykes are outlying products of the volcanic centre which today is marked by Ben More on Mull.

On Barra, the slow erosion of the Lewisian gneiss continued. By this time dinosaurs were abroad, and the landmass that was later to become Barra lay 30 degrees south of the Equator, enjoying a sub-tropical climate. The generally rounded contours of the island's overall shape, with deep-weathered pockets, are a product of the millions of years the ancestral Barra spent drifting slowly northwards through tropical zones. The broad outlines of Barra's landscape were determined long ago.

But one last episode was to come. The changing shore lines of the widening Atlantic, perhaps combined with changes elsewhere and maybe global climate changes, led to a period when ocean circulation failed to redistribute warmth northwards, and the Ice Age was born. Like much of Scotland, Barra would have been affected by the four main cold phases and many smaller oscillations. At times it was covered completely by ice moving west from the Scottish mainland, while at others it probably supported its own small ice cap, or a southern lobe of a Long Island ice cap. But it has to be said that the old, hard rocks were little affected by such trifling matters as several hundred metres of ice grinding over them, and there are no classic glacial erosion features on the island. Some shallow clays and gravels were laid down; a few rock faces steepened, and much of the soil swept away. But Barra was already too gently rounded for the ice to make much difference (Hall 1996:5-11).

Offshore, matters were very different. Deep submarine troughs occur along the east side of the island, reaching up to 250m deep at the south end of the Barra Isles. These have been attributed to glacial erosion, but it is hard to fit into any of the terrestrial evidence, even allowing for softer sediments and weaknesses along the Minch Fault (Sissons 1967:52). On the western edge of the continental shelf, in the Atlantic beyond Barra, vast quantities of glacially-eroded debris carried out by the glaciers from the west of Scotland piled up, subsequently collapsing in vast underwater avalanches down the slope into the depths to create the Barra Fan. (Holmes 1997:92). This is the southernmost of a series of such continental slope deposits which includes those of Norway responsible for the huge, and increasingly well-documented Storegga Slide of about 6000 BC, which created a tsunami responsible for depositing a layer of sand on coastal sites along the eastern Scottish littoral (Smith 2002:468).

Fig. 2 Hebrides and West Highland coast, showing approximate coastline at lowest sea level immediately after last glaciation.

Barra has important claims to the interest of geomorphologists studying relatively recent phenomena. At Cleat[2] a beach of small gravel, plastered on the foot of the cliff at the east end of the bay, appears to date from the period before the last glacial episode. It looks as if the beach was frozen in situ and then buried beneath glacial till from the last ice-cover. Such survivals are rare in Scotland, and the Cleat exposure, though tiny, is important (Gilbertson *et al*, 1996:69) So too are the raised rock platforms visible along the N shore of Vatersay, west of Traigh Varlish, which have also been cited as examples of interglacial features (Gilbertson *et al* 1996:71).

Once the ice had melted, sea levels settled gradually, after much adjustment, to where they are today. It seems certain that for some time, commencing shortly after deglaciation, the whole of the Long Island was a single landmass, although probably always separated from the mainland and the Inner Hebrides. Barra, like the rest of the Long Island and unlike most of mainland Scotland, has remained more or less static relative to sea level since the end of the last glacial period. There are no high raised beaches: if anything the west coast of the island is probably a little lower now than when the ice first melted. This has implications for finding early human settlement, which has often been located on raised coastline sites, for example on Rum or Jura.

Also relevant for settlement was Barra's location: 75 km from the Scottish mainland at Ardnamurchan, and 56 km from Skye. But early arrivals probably avoided long sea crossings, settling Barra across the mere 6.5 km crossing from Eriskay and South Uist, from where the mere 24 km crossing from the Uists to Skye was available[3].

The principal physical changes in the last few thousand years have involved the accumulation on the western side of the island of shell sand, forming dune and beach formations with the machair sand plains so characteristic of the Isles. This sand accumulation, rather than sea level change, has been the principal agent of coastal modification since the first human

---

2   English versions of island place-names have been used above, as these are the forms used in cited sources and may make use of references easier. Cleat is particularly varied, appearing also as Cleit and as Cliad.

3   Evidence, as yet unpublished, has recently emerged for human presence in Harris by 5000 BC, during the later Mesolithic. Clearly the Minch would not have posed an insuperable obstacle for the early Neolithic farmers whose remains are the earliest archaeology so far identified on Barra – see MacLeod, this volume.

settlement of Barra. Both Barra (Eoligarry and the rest of the island) and Vatersay (North and South) were probably composed of pairs of separate islands until wave patterns began to build up the double-backed beaches which today unify them with their other halves (Gilbertson et al, 1996:99). Sandy beaches, while attractive to modern eyes, were not favoured landing places for earlier inhabitants, who would have preferred shingle beaches or small rocky coves where skin, and later wooden, vessels could safely be grounded or anchored.

On land, peat began to accumulate almost as soon as vegetation became established after deglaciation, in rocky basins and low-lying areas including fen slacks behind dune ridges. But the spread of hill, or blanket, peat over the higher slopes probably began a little earlier than 2000 BC, in response to climatic changes involving cooler and damper conditions. The contribution to this of agricultural activity, involving scrub and woodland clearance and soil changes caused by early ploughing and by grazing of domestic stock, remains to be resolved (Brayshay and Edwards 1996:20-26).

The key to Barra's vegetation, both natural and agricultural, lies in the interplay of the acidic peat and relatively immature, post-glacial soils with the encroaching sand. Barra displays the classic Hebridean machair – blacklands – peat sequence, running west to east, although in places the sand has come right across to the east side. The question of the human role in the genesis and maintenance of the distinctive machair landform is much debated in geomorphological circles. It is certainly accepted by botanists that the characteristic *flora* of the machair is maintained through cyclical ploughing, fallowing and fertilising, but the question of the contribution of human use to the *landform* itself seems more moot (Boyd and Boyd 1996: 100-109).

Barra is probably the sandiest of the larger islands of the Outer Hebrides. Crops grown on what are almost pure sands tend to be less reliable. They are very prone to drying, enhanced by strong western winds. It is common for crops, especially potatoes, planted in sandy areas to shoot strongly, and then to be blasted by salt-laden winds. Barley and oats tend to develop weak stems and poor root systems, becoming very prone to windthrow. On the heavier peaty soils, especially where mixed with sand, crops grow more steadily – for example in the Borve valley – but these soils are slow to warm up in the spring and if the summer is poor may never ripen adequately. The most reliable crop on Barra is, and has always been, grass, whether in the form of grazing for livestock or hay. But even here, it is late spring before there is much goodness in the hill grazings, and windy summers can parch the grass.

The troublesome soils and weather of Barra have led to a greater reliance on marine resources than in many other islands, with shellfish and sea fish of considerable importance. Until relatively recent times, most fishing was either from the shore or from small boats working close inshore.

The impact of climate and weather on those taking to the sea was even stronger than those working the land. While there has been little research on Barra itself, we can generalise the patterns from regional data. It seems that around the probable time of the first post-glacial visitors to Barra, the climate was milder than at present (perhaps by about 2 degrees C average summer maximum) and less windy. This benevolent situation persisted through the period assigned to the first farming settlers in the fourth millennium BC. A gradual decline set in, accelerating in the middle to late Bronze Age and accompanied by the increasing growth of peat on land which was becoming more waterlogged, its limited post-glacial fertility largely exhausted. Whatever woodland Barra possessed would have disappeared about this time, either cut for fuel or its regeneration inhibited by grazing animals, increased wind strengths and peat growth. That trees will grow in Barra, when protected from the wind and livestock, is clear to any modern visitor (Boyd and Boyd 1996:135).

There is a tendency, in summarising climate change, to arrive at the BC/AD divide and halt the story, perhaps mentioning the severe cold spell in the late-medieval / early modern period, the Little Ice Age. But it is worth bearing in mind that there was a distinctly pleasant spell of weather lasting several centuries at the end of the first millennium AD – just at the right time to foster the voyages of the Norse settlers who found in Barra, as elsewhere in the Western Isles, a relatively congenial landscape ripe for colonisation.

Today's climate is not a negligible factor in lifestyle and settlement patterns, and it is worth dwelling on. Barra has a humid but equable climate. Its record maximum daily temperature was recorded in 1995, at a modest 26 degrees C (the author is happy to say he was present on that occasion). The temperature differential between winter and summer is among the lowest in Scotland. There is between 110 and 130 centimetres of rain each year, and long-lying snow is a rarity in winter. The sea, like the land, has the lowest summer-winter temperature differential around Scotland, if not in NW Europe, and acts as a temperature regulator for the land[4].

---

4   See Boyd and Boyd 1996:30-50 for a detailed discussion of climate and hydrography, and
    other sections for discussion of their impact on farming and fishing.

The dominant element is the wind. It drives the mechanics of the machair system. The strength of the wind, and the salt it carries, impacts on all activities from farming to fishing. The sheer physical impact of the wind must never be underestimated, and the need to eat more and take breaks when working out of doors in windy conditions puts a rather different perspective on the stereotype of the "lazy crofter".

Shelter from the wind, for crops and for settlement, must always have been a priority; so one might have expected to find early settlement mainly on the sheltered, eastern, side of the island. But the most favoured sites for early (and later) settlement seem to have been the few relatively sheltered pockets on the generally exposed western side. On the east side, only Castlebay seems to be of any great age, and its splendid sheltered harbour may well account for this. But of course, our knowledge of the settlement patterns of early times may be biased, for example by re-use of older sites in more recent times.

There is, however, one very good reason why early settlement might be expected to favour the western side. The soils there are lighter, and easier to work with simple tools. Because clouds tend to build up in westerly winds along the north south rocky hills, the west side of the island receives more sunshine than the east, and also less rain – although it is more windy. The light soils dry out quickly, warming rapidly in the springtime to give a longer growing season than on the east (Boyd and Boyd 1996:38). This must have been a vital advantage in early times and remains so today. So it is perhaps no coincidence that the majority of early settlement sites have been located towards the western side.

To conclude: with geology two-thirds as old as the Earth itself and weather which changes every hour, to understand the prehistory and history of Barra, to contemplate why modern life is as it is, and to look into the future, all require a sound grasp on the physical geography of the island. While physical factors may not uniquely determine human options, they certainly narrow down the possibilities. Making a living, or simply surviving, on islands requires a close working knowledge of the natural world. Understanding human relationships with the natural environment is the key to understanding human life on Barra, both ancient and modern.

References

Boyd, J.M. and Boyd, I.L. (1996) *The Hebrides – A Natural Tapestry*, Edinburgh.

Brayshay, B. and Edwards, K. (1996) 'Late-glacial and Holocene vegetational history of South Uist and Barra' in Gilbertson, D., Kent, M. and Grattan, J. (eds.) *The Outer Hebrides: the Last 14,000 Years,* Sheffield.

Fettes, D.J., Mendum, J.R, Smith, D.I. and Watson, J.V. (1992) *Geology of the Outer Hebrides,* London.

Gilbertson, D., Grattan, J., Pyatt, B. and Schwenninger, J-L. (1996) 'The Quaternary geology of the coasts of the islands of the Southern Outer Hebrides' in Gilbertson, D., Kent, M. and Grattan, J. (eds.) *The Outer Hebrides: the Last 14,000 Years,* Sheffield.

Hall, A. (1996) 'Quaternary geomorphology of the Outer Hebrides' in Gilbertson, D., Kent, M. and Grattan, J. (eds.) *The Outer Hebrides: the Last 14,000 Years,* Sheffield.

Holmes, R. (1997) 'Quaternary Stratigraphy: the Offshore Record' in Gordon, J.G. (ed.) *Reflections on the Ice Age in Scotland,* Glasgow.

Sissons, J.B. (1967) *The Evolution of Scotland's Scenery,* Edinburgh.

Smith, D.E. (2002) 'The Storegga Disaster', *Current Archaeology* 179 (May 2002), London.

Kisimul Castle and the Origins of Hebridean Galley-Castles: Preliminary Thoughts

Ian R. Macneil

Introduction

INVESTIGATING the origins[1] of Kisimul Castle (Figure 1) reveals major problems in the historiography of Hebridean castles.

- Debatable assumptions commonly become foundations for conclusions with little or no recognition that they are debatable. Indeed they do so even without recognition that they are assumptions and not demonstrated facts.
- Too often information is analysed with inadequate attention to context.
- The need for comprehensive systematic analysis and studies is ignored.
- Narrow and historically inappropriate frames of reference all too often distort analyses.

The upshot of all this is that conclusions based on evidence justifying only possibilities are confidently stated as probabilities or even as virtual certainties.

Four propositions: In response to the foregoing, this paper advances four propositions:

1. All debatable assumptions must be recognised as such and then verified through specific explanation if possible and if not, discarded.
2. Information must never be analysed out of full context.

---

[1] Origins means such things as: Who had the castle built? Who were the actual builders? For what purposes was it built? How are those purposes reflected in its general and precise location? its design? materials used? What technologies and skills were required? What cultural sources and influences affected all such matters? When was it built?

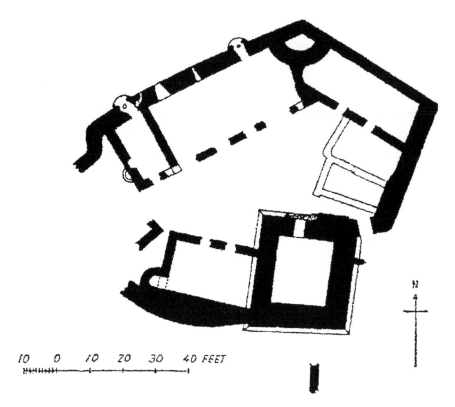

Figure 1: Kisimul Castle c1860s after extensive 'quarrying'.
(Copyright Robert L Macneil, Ian R Macneil.)

   3. Sound analysis of debatable issues can be based only on comprehensive studies, not on bits and pieces of selected information.

   4. Prevailing frames of reference distort analysis of the origins of many Hebridean Castles, and require re-placement with more historically sound approaches.

Three of these boil down to the need for more science and less anecdote in the historiography of Hebridean castles. The fourth deals with more substantive issues.

   Justifying these four propositions is my sole aim here. They are properly judged, I believe, not on where they lead respecting the origins of Hebridean Castles, but on how well-founded they are in fact and principle.

Hebridean Galley-Castles: *Hebridean Galley-Castle* is a coined term and therefore calls for definition:

- *Hebrides* and *Hebridean* include not only the Norse *Sudreys*, but also the mainland adjacent to the Sudreys.
- A *galley* is any galley-type boat, but is typically Norse, Hebridean, or Irish.
- A *castle* is any lime-mortar or drystone structure combining residence and defence of the period 800 to 1600, far longer than in conventional definitions.
- A *galley-castle* is any castle close enough to the sea directly or by portage to have been significantly influenced by the existence of galleys when they were a dominant military factor. Most castles in both the Hebridean islands and on Hebridean mainland shores are galley-castles.

I DEBATABLE ASSUMPTIONS

Verification of debatable assumptions; Scottish Diffusionism

Assumptions are as essential in studying Hebridean Castles as in any other human endeavour. They must, however, be dealt with properly:

- All assumptions that are possibly debatable must be explicitly revealed as such.
- All debatable assumptions must be either justified by specific explanation or discarded.

Revelation and verification of assumptions is, of course, no more than an essential element of the scientific approach to any subject.

Scottish Diffusionism

Unfortunately, untested debatable assumptions about Hebridean Castles rival the Highland midge in numbers. Foremost, and the parent of a host of other untested assumptions, is the orthodox analysis of Hebridean Castles which I call Scottish Diffusionism:

Conventional analysis of Hebridean Castles typically assumes, without discussion, that they are Scottish. This Scoto-centric approach automatically tends towards late dating. It appears to assume a diffusion of cultural influences from the outcome of the Battle of Hastings in 1066. These moved northward by land to what is now eastern-central Scotland. They then radiated slowly out from that hub like snails along the spokes of a cart-wheel to the distant parts of what is now modern Scotland, but much of which was not Scotland then. The last places the snails reached were those farthest from the hub, places like the Western Isles, Caithness, and Orkney and Shetland. Neither snails nor anything else of significance travelled along the rim of the wheel independently of the spokes.

A story goes that while Donald Dewar was First Minister he flew to Stornoway and was then driven to a house in a small village in Harris. There he was introduced to an old lady. Tired from the long trip, he said: 'My, you live in a remote place.' The old lady fixed a sharp eye on him and said: 'Remote from where?' That is, of course, the key question respecting Hebridean castles; Scottish Diffusionism simply assumes it means remote from eastern-central Scotland.

Other common debatable assumptions
Other common debatable assumptions include the following:
- **No indigenous evolution**
  No indigenous evolution was involved in the development of Hebridean Castles.
- **Late unless proven early**
  A castle is late unless proven to be early:
      This castle is very hard to date;
      Thus it must be very very late.
- **Hebrideans were too backward to build castles at early periods**
  The people of the Hebrides were so backward that they could not have built even extremely primitive castles at an early period. This view reached a sorry peak in 1927 with W. Mackay Mackenzie, Secretary of the Royal Commission. Rejecting early dates for castles in the West Highlands and Isles, he wrote:

  > At a time when memorial effigies in the south were being cut in a complete outfit of plate armour, those in the west show only the ancient quilted coat with cape of mail. So too in the case of western castles (Mackenzie 1927:42).

This assumption of Hebridean backwardness is splendidly self-proving: when the Hebrideans did start castle-building, their castles were, of course, hopelessly archaic. Thus, Mackenzie wrote of Kisimul Castle after dating it as mid-15th century:

> Our special interest is in the fact that it was as old-fashioned in style as the quilted coat which continued to be the body armour of the island chiefs in the days of armour plate. (Ibid. :164)

What a marvellous picture! Here is Macneil of Barra in the full body plate armour of the mounted knight, being lowered by a large crane onto the stern of Kisimul's Galley. There he stands – magnificent and immobilised – as the galley sails out into the Minch to meet the foe. And there he stands – magnificent and immobilised – as the battle rages. And still he stands – magnificent and immobilised – as the galley returns triumphant to Kisimul where he is winched off and carried victorious into the Great Hall.

Pace Mackenzie, but quilted coats with mail did not cease to be state-of-the-art in galley warfare just because elsewhere knights fighting in medieval armies and mounted on great war-horses had adopted full body-plate armour.

Upon hearing of Mackenzie's nonsense my wife – who has lived in a galley-castle – said: 'Yes, and just think of the rust!'

The effigies of obsolete body armour are quite literally the sole evidence Mackenzie offers of Hebridean backwardness in general and of Barra backwardness in particular.

These days no one would be so politically incorrect as to express openly such views or perhaps even to realise that they held them. Nonetheless, one still runs across a whiff of assumptions of Hebridean backwardness in a phenomenon described forty years ago by Stewart Cruden responding to Mackenzie on effigies:

> In these and similar observations we sense that the possibility of early date is considered with alarm and dismissed with relief, and we feel the author's growing confidence as he transfers his attention to features of unquestionably later date (Cruden 1960:15-16).

This notion of Hebridean backwardness also reflects the assumption already mentioned that ideas took decades or centuries to move and be absorbed from one place to another. Respecting matters of political and military importance to warlords, however, nothing is likely to be farther from the truth. Hebridean warlords were a highly political and aggressive lot; they were equipped with galleys making quick work of the relatively short distances between Hebridean islands or even farther afield.

For example, the latest that successful mid-twelfth century Hebridean warlords might have learned of the castle built on Wyre in Orkney by Kolbein Hruga was a sailing season after its erection around 1150. After all, that castle dominates one of the two primary sea lanes from the Hebrides to Norway. Nor are they likely to have been unaware of Castle Rushen in the Isle of Man as soon as it was erected. Their power and prestige – to say nothing of their lives – depended upon such knowledge. Only fifty years earlier King Magnus of Norway had laid waste to the Hebrides, and in this very era Somerled was fighting Godred for the Isle of Man. Nor was mere knowledge of military developments enough; their success and lives depended equally on prompt and effective responses. Whether one of those responses was to build a castle in Castlebay we do not know; that it might have been we do know.

Maybe this completely unverified assumption of Hebridean backwardness has disappeared from the conscious hearts and minds of modern archaeologists and historians. Nonetheless, it lies buried like anthrax spores in countless patches throughout much of the golden mountain of historical and archaeological information we all mine so deeply in conducting our modern studies.

Overall effect = late dating
The overall effect of all these unverified assumptions is by no means random. Each leans in only one direction: the late-dating of Hebridean Castles.

No historiography basing late-dating on these assumptions is scientifically sound.

Verifying debatable assumptions in existing work

Obviously it is essential that people doing new work in this area adhere to basic scientific principles by verifying their assumptions.

What, however, about verification of the huge body of unexamined and debatable assumptions in existing work? Many for example, dominate individual studies of castles in the 1928 Inventory of Skye and the Outer Islands, and again in the later Orkney & Shetland and Argyll inventories. Naturally, those valuable and indispensable studies have been a foundation for much other work, bringing their assumptions right along with them.

We can hardly expect everyone to lay down their shovels and/or pens to engage in a full-scale examination of these assumptions throughout the vast body of existing studies. It is, however, not too much to expect serious scholars to deal properly with all possibly debatable assumptions in any existing study they intend to use in their own work. This means:

- Carefully teasing out the assumptions in the earlier work.
- Either supporting debatable assumptions with specific and well-founded explanation or discarding them.
- Re-evaluating the earlier work after discarding unsupportable assumptions.
- Relying on the earlier work only to the extent still justified after the foregoing.

It is barely necessary to add that, having limited the use of existing work in this manner, modern scholars need to be astute to avoid introducing additional unverified and debatable assumptions into their own work.

II CONTEXTUAL ANALYSIS

Introduction

Turning now to my second proposition: Information must never be analysed out of full context. This applies both to re-evaluation of our existing corpus of information and to the development of new information.

Indigenous input

A telling remark was made not long ago in a television program on Mine Howe in Orkney: 'The single most important thing in understanding a structure is considering what was already there when it was built.' Unfortunately, such respect for context tends to be sadly lacking in the historiography of Hebridean castles. As already suggested, conventional analysis typically assumes away indigenous context. Thus Kisimul, for example, is treated like the first motor car in Barra in 1926: A new cultural artefact coming entirely from abroad. The main concession to indigenous input typically is acceptance that the castles are made largely of local stone.

Analysis of any type of structure ignoring the indigenous *status quo* is generally indefensible; it is particularly malevolent in the case of Hebridean Castles. They were built in areas with a rich history of promontory fortifications, duns, and brochs. Moreover, the Norse penetration introduced a vigourous, intelligent, and aggressive new people. These people were faced with a challenging new environment of existing fortifications and other structures made of stone, to say nothing of a great lack of their accustomed building material, wood. Meanwhile, of course, the existing population was subjected to the challenge of the Norse. Could the resulting cultural cauldron have been so totally lacking in impact on the development of residential fortifications that we can afford to ignore the possibility? Hardly.

Nonetheless, conventional scholarship overlooks altogether structures not fitting orthodox definitions of castles, many of which may nonetheless be pertinent to indigenous evolution. Consider Dun Ban on an islet in Loch Caravat in North Uist. It has what may have been a dun wall, but is lime-mortared, has a square corner uncharacteristic of duns, and had a medieval building inside. From the plan and imaginary reconstruction (Figure 2), Dun Ban gives every appearance of being an early, low-curtain-walled castle. The 1928 Inventory notes that it has 'features in common with the castles of the mainland, with which the builder was evidently familiar.' (RCAHMS 1928:29) Nonetheless, the Inventory characterises it as a late dun, not as a castle.

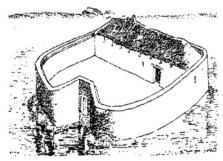

Figure 2: Dun Ban, Loch Caravat. (RCAHMS, 1928.)

Another borderline structure is Dun Raouill on an islet in Loch Druidibeg in South Uist (Figure 3). The 1928 Inventory denominated it as a dun, and described it as 'of a very uncommon type.' (RCAHMS 1928:380) Figure 3 reveals this to be a considerable understatement. The very originality of this structure cries out for study of indigenous roles in the development of Hebridean Castles.

Nonetheless, so far as I can ascertain neither Dun Ban nor Dun Raouill has ever been considered in mainstream studies as possibly pertinent to the origins of Hebridean medieval castles.

If structures such as these are overlooked, we may be quite certain that ordinary drystone duns built or occupied after 800 will also be ignored.

Only if indigenous input is entirely ruled out can any of these structures be safely ignored in the comprehensive studies needed to determine the origin of Hebridean castles.

Unfortunately, this lack of attention to context permeates many areas of investigation. Two illustrations are charters and John of Fordun, both having played major roles in dates assigned to, *inter alia*, Kisimul.

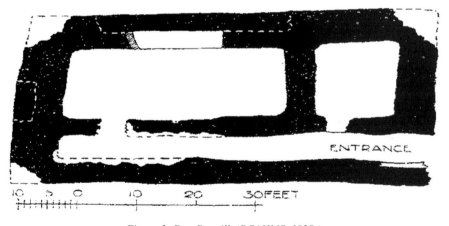

Figure 3: Dun Raouill. (RCAHMS, 1928.)

Charters

Where a charter names a castle, presumption of its contemporaneous existence without further contextual analysis may often be safe. What, however, may and may not be properly inferred from non-mention of a castle in charters? This question can arise in a number of ways.

Charter mentions one or more castles, but not the one in question

The strongest case for inferring the non-existence of a castle is where a charter mentions one or more castles, but not the one in question. Mention of at least one purportedly shows the importance of castles, giving rise to an inference that all castles in all the lands granted would naturally have been mentioned. There is even a legal maxim for this proposition: *Expressio unius, exclusio alterius.* Like all legal maxims it is hazardous to the truth when used out of context.

Thus, for example, to the extent that it was common in Hebridean charters to mention some but not all castles then the inference of non-existence of an unmentioned one is weakened. How common was it? This question can be answered only by comprehensive examination of all such charters available to us. Nonetheless, while this argument is not uncommon, I have yet to see such an examination.

Even more important in this situation is internal contextual examination of the document itself. Consider, for example, the Indenture of 1354 between John of Islay and John of Lorn, which among many things involved quitclaims to Mull and Tiree, as well as the Isle of Coll (Munro 1986:5-8).

The indenture explicitly mentions three castles – the two Cairnaborgs and Dun Chonnuill – all on small out-islands in important seaways. Four castles go unmentioned: Breacachadh Castle on Coll, Aros and Duart Castles on Mull and the tower on Tiree mentioned a decade or two later by John of Fordun.

Turner & Dunbar have drawn the inference that Breacachadh Castle on Coll did not exist in 1354 because it goes unmentioned in this indenture. Since they failed to make a thorough contextual examination of the indenture, they failed to notice that the same inference applies with equal force to Aros, Duart and a tower on Tiree. Unless the authors were willing to deny the existence of these other castles at that time – highly unlikely – it was entirely illogical to assert on these grounds that Breacachadh Castle did not exist in 1354.

Charter is silent

It is equally unsound to infer the non-existence of a castle from a charter mentioning no castles at all. Only a comprehensive study showing that Hebridean charters virtually always mentioned extant castles could justify such an inference. There is none.

Moreover, local context must also be considered. For example, the 1427 charter of Barra to Gilleonan Macneil contains no mention of Kisimul. As well as Barra, however, the charter granted to Macneil the lands of Baegastallis –

now called Boisdale – in South Uist. That name itself – apparently Gaelic for Castle Bay – constitutes evidence of the existence of a castle there at that time. In addition, extensive remains in Boisdale of a medieval castle, Castle Calvay, also raise the possibility that the charter granted another castle besides Kisimul without mentioning its existence. Nonetheless, this charter has played a major role in support of post-1427 datings of Kisimul.

No charters

The very weakest case for equating non-mention with non-existence is where no charters at all are known during the entire period when a castle may or may not have been extant. Nonetheless, the absence of charters is not uncommonly presented as an element supporting late dating. This too is done with no examination of important contextual questions. These include among others: First, how extensive was the use of charters at all in Hebridean waters at the pertinent periods? Second, how many charters which may have existed survived sufficiently long for knowledge of them to come to modern eyes?

In sum, reasoning from a negative is always a dangerous business; in the case of Hebridean castles and charters, it is downright foolhardy.

John of Fordun

Much of what has been said about charters applies equally to other contemporary historical sources, one of the most important of which is John of Fordun.

Introduction

John of Fordun's *Chronica Gentis Scottorum*, written around the 1370s, contains a chapter – all of a page and a half – entitled *De insulis Scotiae divisis ab insulis Orcadibus*. Another chapter listing 39 Orkney islands by name only follows. A full investigation of Fordun's two chapters is beyond the scope of this paper. Considering their context will, however, suffice before weighing what, if any, conclusions may properly be drawn from Fordun's identifying a number of castles and towers in the first of these chapters.

As the title indicates, Fordun's chapter is a list of islands he calls islands of Scotland apart from the Orkneys. Fordun identified 46, although he made clear that the list was incomplete. Included among the 46 are the Isle of Man and Rathlin Island. This leaves 44 islands of modern Scotland, 8 in the Clyde, 34 in the Hebrides, two on the north coast, one of which – in a rare mistake – is actually a peninsula, and none on the east coast.

Purpose of the two chapters on islands

Considerable puzzlement exists about the reasons behind these chapters. There is nothing else like them in his Chronicle, which is largely a history book, both ancient and modern, not a geography.

I believe both chapters are political. Although Norway owned the Orkneys at the time, Scotland had an acquisitive eye on them. Fordun's including the Isle of Man and Rathlin as two of Scotia's islands also can be explained only as a political ploy. And finally, while legally the Hebrides had belonged to Scotland for a century, it would be long indeed before the King of Scots acquired any firm hegemony over them. Hence the desire in a nationalistic work to list the islands and, where it was easily available, provide scattered information about some of them – rather like a wolf marking what it hopes will be its territory. There is no mention whatever of the unquestionably Scottish east coast islands where no political propaganda was needed.

Not a comprehensive gazetteer

Be that as it may, Fordun's chapter was neither intended to be nor is a comprehensive gazetteer of the islands. Fordun supplies only names for 16 of the 44 Scottish islands. This full one-third of his list includes Kerrera, Coll, Skye, and Lewis. Another 14 islands generate one item of information each; three are the most for any island. These items of information fall into three categories.

Miscellaneous items

The most common – 23 – are a miscellaneous assortment. They include natural information – nearby whirlpools and whales, hilly character, and the like, the size or length of an island, location relative to other islands, sparse population, good sport, and fertility.

No one would dream of arguing that any of this miscellaneous information was intended to be a comprehensive listing of anything.

Ecclesiastical items

The second category consists of 14 ecclesiastical items. Most of these identify buildings – cells, chapels, monasteries, a parish church, and an abbey. At least four refer to sanctuary or *refugium*; standing alone this may or may not refer to a building. One reference simply locates the Episcopal See of Argyll on Lismore.

Examination of the Argyll inventories reveals readily enough that Fordun's ecclesiastical sites constitute only a sample and not an exhaustive list. Omissions almost certainly include: Pennygown (Mull), Kilvickean (Mull), Soroby (Tiree), Cill an Ailein (Mull), Kilchattan (Luing), and St. Mary's and St. Oran's (Iona). Many others throughout the islands are quite likely to have been extant in the 1370s.

Secular buildings

Fordun's third category consists of 13 secular buildings, or 14 if his reference to *Insula* Tyreym is judged to be a reference to *Castrum* Tyreym.

Two of these secular buildings were mansions of the Lords of the Isles in Islay, three were royal castles on Arran and Bute, seven, if we count Castle Tioram, were named castles on Hebridean islands, and two were unnamed towers on Hebridean islands.

Fordun's other specifically-named Hebridean castles were, to use modern names, (1) Dunyvaig on Islay, (2) Dun Chonnuil in the Garvellachs, (3) Duart and (4) Aros on Mull, (5) Cairnaborg, and (6) probably Borve in Benbecula.

His two unnamed towers were on Tiree and Thorset. Contrary to both Skene and the modern editor of Bower's *Scotichronicon*, I see no reason to think that Fordun's *Insula* Thorset is anything other than Torsa, a tidal island of Luing about a mile long. Fordun's name for the island – Thor's Seat – and Torsa – Thor's Island – are virtually interchangeable. And there is a medieval tower there.   ·

Just as with the other categories of Fordun's information, it is evident that the Hebridean island castles and towers identified did not constitute an exhaustive list. At least three more almost certainly existed: Achadun and Coeffin on Lismore, and Dunvegan on Skye. This is, however, a minimum. What, for example, of other castles which may be mid-14th century or earlier on two of the islands about which Fordun provided no information whatever: Lewis and Skye? On Lewis, Stornoway and Dun Eistean are obvious possibilities. On Skye, apart from Dunvegan, three come quickly to mind: Knock, Dunscaith, and Duntulm. Nor can we afford to ignore other possibilities such as Dun Ara and Moy on Mull, Kisimul in Barra, Calvay in Uist, and Castle Mestag on Stroma. Indeed, freed of the blinders of Scottish Diffusionism there may be dozens of then existing island castles Fordun failed to mention.

Fordun's identification of the castles and towers he does locate are useful to show their existence in the 1370s. But his identifications simply cannot logically be used as even the slightest evidence of the non-existence of other castles.

Misusing Fordun as a list of castles

In sum, the only list Fordun made was a list of islands. What he said about them – when he said anything at all – created no lists of anything. They were simply bits and pieces of information he had acquired. He had more extensive bits and pieces in some categories – ecclesiastical and secular buildings – than in others. But in no category did he create a list, much less an exhaustive list.

In spite of all this, starting no later than the RCAHMS 1928 Inventory of the Outer Isles and Skye, it has become commonplace to call the castles and towers Fordun identified on various islands a *list* of castles. The so-called *list* is then used as strong evidence of the non-existence in the 1370s or even later of any non-included castle. Even though illogical and a corruption of what Fordun was doing, this continues to be done and continues to distort the history of Hebridean castles.

III COMPREHENSIVE STUDIES

My third proposition is that sound analysis of debatable issues can be based only on comprehensive studies, not on bits and pieces of selected information.

Meaning of *Comprehensive*: The appropriate set

Comprehensive here means studies starting with a set *including at a minimum all possible* Hebridean castles as defined earlier.

Castles alone not enough

Examining only castles is, however, by no means adequate for truly comprehensive studies. For many purposes, for example studying the use or non-use of lime-mortar in the Hebrides, all stone structures of the era – not just castles – require consideration.

Geographic enlargement

Moreover, geographic enlargement is also required. To be sufficiently comprehensive, inquiries must include all structures outside the Hebrides which might have influenced building in the Hebrides. The most immediate areas to consider are Orkney, Sutherland, Caithness, and Isle of Man and others, such as the Clyde, Galloway, Norway, and Ireland, and other parts of modern Scotland. The value of any study failing to go at least this far is subject to serious limitations. A really comprehensive approach would also include: Northwest England to Wales, Wales including Anglesey, Southwest England to Land's End, the rest of Scandinavia, Northern Europe outside Scandinavia, Normandy, Provence, other parts of France, and the East.

Individual-castle analysis – selective comparisons

I know of no single comprehensive study along the foregoing lines. Instead we typically find analyses of individual castles based on comparisons with selective examples of other castles. This selective-comparison technique commonly determines both which castles and which features are compared.

There can be little objection to using selective examples respecting undebatable matters; indeed reasonably concise studies demand doing so. But using selective examples respecting debatable issues is simply unacceptable in any scientific analysis. Distortion of evidence and conclusions in such a process is unavoidable.

Moreover, a particular problem arises when comparative studies of individual objects are carried out repeatedly over long periods of time. Each conclusion about one subject of study becomes a brick in the foundation of the next study. Before long a substantial structure of conclusions exists locking the entire body of learning into a conventional, but potentially unsound, intellectual edifice.

Whatever unverified assumptions underlie the early stages of this process soon become proven to be 'true' by its self-fulfilling nature. And the truer they are perceived to be the less need anyone will see to verify them. This, I believe, has happened to the study of Hebridean castles for nearly a century. Of course, the unverified assumptions have never in fact been verified by this process; they remain just as problematic as ever.

So far as I can tell there is little perception that this selection problem exists respecting Hebridean castles. There seems to be widespread and basic failure to recognise that in this kind of scholarly enterprise sound analysis requires one of only two possible courses of action. One is to examine the entire comprehensive set. The other – to be used where the whole set is too large – is to use statistically adequate random sampling.

Remedies

A number of things can be done to remedy this problem. In more or less ascending order of difficulty they are:

- **Recognition**

  Simply to recognise that the problem exists and that it affects a large corpus of scholarship.

- **Recognising limitations of past selectivity**

  To recognise that past dominance of selectivity imposes severe limitations on the definiteness of conclusions that may be properly drawn from existing studies of Hebridean castles.

- **Future studies comprehensive**

  To engage where at all feasible only in either across-the-board or genuinely random-selection studies respecting debatable subjects.

- **Where not feasible recognise limitations**

  Where that is not feasible, to make crystal clear the nature and limitations of the selective study adopted instead and to refrain from stating conclusions unjustified in light of those limitations.

- **Revisiting existing historiography**

  Finally, to revisit the existing corpus of scholarship to ascertain what has and what has not escaped problems resulting from the selective approach. The sheer volume of such a task is enough to strike fear into anyone thinking about doing it, even in little pieces. Nonetheless, initial steps to remedy the problem may not be as daunting as they seem. The Royal Commission inventories of Argyll, Orkney and Shetland, and Skye and the Outer Islands are both the most important and the most easily investigated on this score. Moreover their very nature permits investigation in small bites.

Dimensions of appropriate set

This set of possible Hebridean Castles has many dimensions, each with a wide range. There is, however, a strong tendency for scholarship to focus on the easy end of each dimension and to neglect the more difficult end. This is a variant of what the late Graham Ritchie referred to in another context as the Honeypot Syndrome. If we are ever to get closer to the truth about the origins of Hebridean Castles it is essential that the whole of each range be examined, not just the obvious honeypots.

- **Degree of Prominence – Calendar-Castles and Shadow-Castles**

One dimension is prominence. At the easy end are Calendar (or Postcard) Castles known to everyone, such as Duart, Dunvegan, and especially Eilean Donan.

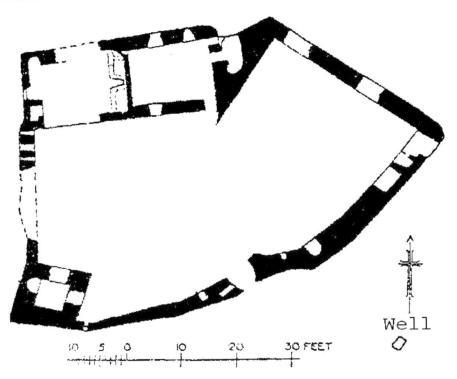

Well

Figure 4: Castle Calvay. (RCAHMS, 1928.)

At the difficult end are Shadow-Castles that both the world at large and historiography have left living in peaceful obscurity. There are countless of these, including Mestag on Stroma and Castle Holm (or Strom) in Shetland.

Castle Calvay, an important castle lying less than 16 miles from Kisimul, is just such a Shadow-Castle. As Figure 4 shows, Calvay is a curtain wall castle lacking a tower of any significance. This is a form generally believed to be that of the earliest Hebridean castles. As already mentioned there is place-name evidence suggesting Calvay's existence in 1427.

Calvay and Kisimul were visited just two days apart in the preparation of the 1928 Inventory. The Inventory account of Kisimul mentions two similarities between it and Calvay: the small towers in the northern wall and the 'peculiarity' of bedding slabs on edge. Compare Figures 1 and 4 for others.

Ever since the 1928 Inventory, Calvay has, so far as I can tell, simply sat there and been ignored. Its relevance to the origins of Kisimul Castle was completely ignored in both the 1928 Inventory and the detailed official study of Kisimul published in 1978.

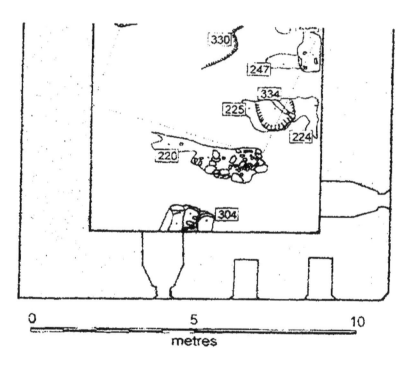

*Figure 5: Carrick Castle. Pre-1350 remains of prior structure. Lime-mortar wall (No. 220)
and clay-bonded wall (No. 304). (Copyright Gordon Ewart & Fiona Baker.)*

Current existence/non-existence and certainty of original existence

Another dimension affecting comprehensive studies is survival or even existence at any time. Hebridean Castles range from largely extant – Dunvegan – to totally lost – Stornoway. So too they also range from castles which certainly once existed to castles so lost in the mists of the past that they may or may not be mere figments of imagination. Almost as deep in the shadows are scanty remnants long since buried in later structures. Figure 5 shows such remnants at Carrick, Loch Goil, a galley-castle, albeit non-Hebridean.

The only difference between a long lost castle and one still with us is how much or how little we can know about it. That, however, is no excuse for not using what we do know in scholarly studies. For example, the fact that one remnant at Carrick is lime-mortar and the other clay-bonded could be quite important in any comprehensive study of those two building techniques.

- **Extent studied**

Another dimension affecting comprehensive studies is the extent to which individual castles have been studied. The honeypot includes those which have been excavated and studied to a fare-thee-well – Tioram comes to mind. They are, however, not the slightest bit more important for scholarly studies than castles which have at most been measured and casually photographed, or sometimes not even that. And yet scholarly attention tends to focus on the well-studied while ignoring the others.

- **Extensiveness of historical roles**

Hebridean Castles also range from major participants in known history – Duart, Duniveg, Dunstaffnage, Mingarry, Tioram – to those having little or no currently known role – Dun Ara (Mull) and Dun Ban in Loch Caravat and again Calvay. Nonetheless, castles without a known history are just as important in seeking the origins of Hebridean Castles as those with it; they are left out of consideration only at the peril of the truth. After all, those who built Hebridean castles had no idea which would become historic and which would not.

- **Types of Structures**

The nature of the structures required to be studied as possible Hebridean castles is broad indeed. The honeypot end, of course, includes all the Calendar-Castles. Also reasonably near that end are countless others, such as Bheagram in Uist, Braal in Caithness, and Dunscaith in Skye, structures that no one would deny are medieval castles.

At the other end of the range are structures failing to fit conventional definitions, such as drystone duns either built or occupied after 800. As noted earlier, ignoring of such structures is also a denial of indigenous influence on the origins of Hebridean Castles.

Subjects needing comprehensive studies

Determining the appropriate set for study is the first step in the comprehensive study of any subject. Having suggested how broad that set needs to be respecting Hebridean Castles I turn now to the wide range of general subjects in need of comprehensive study.

Such studies are lacking not only of whole castles, but also of a vast array of particular aspects which may be significant in determining these origins. Subjects needing comprehensive studies may be grouped roughly under four headings:

Physical: Construction and Archaeological Finds[2]
Historical Evidence[3]
Functions[4]
Relations[5]

---

2   A virtually unlimited number of typological and other architecture details and types of archaeological finds. For example: (1) Initial uses of lime-mortar construction (a) in the Hebrides, (b) elsewhere along the Norse-Celtic Seaways, (c) pertinent parts of Scotland, (d) everywhere else that might have had a current impact in the Hebrides; (2) Use of vitrifaction and clay-mortar; (3) Particular construction peculiarities, such as (a) laying stones on edges or end (Kisimul, Breacachadh, Calvay, The Wirk), (b) failures to bond walls (Kisimul), (c) distinctive patterns of large stones and small stones (St. Magnus Church, Eglisay, Caisteal nan Con, Torsa, Kisimul), (d) wicker vaulting (Dunollie, Tioram, Irish); (4) materials and their sources, particularly apparently non-local materials, e.g. green slate (e.g. Kisimul, Tioram, Castle Sinclair(?))

3   (1) Careful study of usefulness and limits of (a) charter and license evidence and (b) John of Fordun's and other identifications of castles, particularly to prove the non-existence of castles; (2) Traditions, usefulness and limits (a) Danish, Viking forts and (b) Individual castles; (3) Place-name evidence, e.g. which '-sdale,' etc. endings = a'chaisteal?

4   Relative to (1) Sea-borne commerce, communications, and warfare, particularly as relates to galleys; (2) All aspects of location, including inter alia relations to location of other castles and topographical locations; (3) Castle structure, both generally and particular features; (4) Galley facilities – galley footprints – and relationship to castle/castles.

5   (1) Indigenous forerunners (a) as such and (b) modifications and use during galley-era; (2) Possible geographic relations: (a) Norse-Celtic Seaways: (i) Scandanavia, (ii) Orkney, (iii) Sutherland & Caithness, (iv) Clyde, (v) Galloway, (vi) Isle of Man, (vii) Ireland, (viii) West England to Wales, (ix) Welsh, (x) Southwest England to Land's End; (b) Scotland (outwith Hebrides and Hebridean-Mainland); (c) Other possible non- Scottish influences: (i) Northern Europe outside Scandinavia, (ii) Normandy, (iii) Provence, (iv) Other French, (v) Eastern; (3) Particular historical relations, e.g. Somerled.

A few illustrations and comments will make the non-exhaustive lists of these four types in the footnotes more comprehensible:

Physical

Absolutely crucial is a truly comprehensive study of the uses of lime-mortar construction. Is it, for example, absurd to think that any lime-mortar masonry was laid in the Hebrides before 1100? 1000? 900? 800? 700? If so, why? Only a comprehensive study can answer those and other vital questions about what is possible and what is not possible respecting the use of lime-mortar. It is absolutely essential to involve highly experienced masons and other workers with stone in any study involving masonry – like war these studies are too important to be left to the Generals.

Historical

A useful historical study would be a comprehensive examination of topographical names ending in '-sdale' or the equivalent, to see which ones may mean the Gaelic *a'chaisteal* rather than the Norse *dal*.

Functions

A useful comprehensive study of functions would be of the locations of these castles relative to sea-borne commerce, communications, and warfare, particularly as relates to galleys. Among many things this should include a comprehensive admirality-chart-oriented study of sailing times, a project suggested by Donald McWhannell.

Relations

Last, but by no means least, relations. As already emphasised, all comprehensive studies of physical and historical evidence and of functions must be tightly linked to all possible relations possibly affecting them. This includes most emphatically relations both indigenous and outside the Hebrides in all directions, not just directly east. But in addition comprehensive studies of particular relations as such are needed. Two examples will suffice.

- Studies of location relative to other galley-castles is vital.
- A large number of Hebridean castles were possibly built in the mid-12th century. Is there a relationship between this and Somerled's empire-building?

IV REVISIONS OF PREVAILING FRAMES OF REFERENCE

Introduction

The three propositions advanced so far have all addressed the need for more scientific rigour in studies of the origins of Hebridean castles. Although my particular application of them will no doubt be criticised, the propositions themselves are hardly subject to challenge.

I now turn to something rather different: the need to revise prevailing frames of reference relating to these castles. I believe that the changes proposed will help us greatly in dealing with everything to do with their origins.

More specifically, I believe we need to revise the way we think about Hebridean Castles in terms of three frames of reference: (1) their functions as galley-castles, (2) the appropriate contextual time-frame, and (3) location.

1) FUNCTIONS: GALLEY-CASTLES

Usual castle functions

Like other castles, Hebridean Galley-Castles functioned as residences and centres for the wide range of economic-political-administrative-legal-military activities in which the residents were involved. They created space hoped to be secure from dangers such as common everyday pilferage on up to major military attack. This enclosure also made it easy to regulate who came and left – or did not leave, dedicated space for prisons being common. They were likely to be homes to a range of crafts and manufacture, either inside or nearby. Many may have been entrepots for trade. They were centres for hospitality, especially important in Gaelic and Norse cultures. And unquestionably they served as symbols of power and prestige.

Domination by the galley

In one respect, however, these castles differed from countless other medieval castles.

Everything about them was in symbiotic relationship with the galley. They were built when and where galleys and their crews dominated commerce, communication, culture, and military and political life. These galleys and their use were inevitably a primary influence on everything to do with the castles from start to finish. Hence the term galley- castles.

Trying to comprehend Hebridean castles respecting trade and communication without focusing on galleys is like trying to understand *amazon.com*'s warehouses without thinking about airplanes, lorries, vans, telephones, computers or the internet, to say nothing of roller-skates. So too, trying to comprehend their military aspects without focusing on galleys is like trying to understand the Siegfried or Maginot Lines without considering aircraft, high explosive artillery, tanks, machine guns, telephones, or radios.

Finding recognition in conventional studies of the role of the galley respecting Hebridean castles is rare indeed. About the most is generally some reference to a nearby galley berth.

Galley should be the central focus

I believe that when proper and full consideration is given to the roles of galleys, it will be seen that *the galley must be a central focus* of our thinking about anything to do with any castle built in the Hebrides or Hebridean-Mainland between 800 and 1500 or even later. It would be an exaggeration to say that the primary purpose of these castles was to serve as Galley Terminals. Nonetheless, thinking of them in that way would be a useful corrective to the all-too-common approach of largely or even totally ignoring their relation to galleys.

2) CONTEXTUAL TIME-FRAME

Galley dominance dictates dates of *c*800 – *c*1600

The dominance of the galley leads directly to the need to commence the study of origins of Hebridean Castles no later than about 800 at the very latest. It was then, or more precisely in the prior decade, that the galley is first known to have made a major impact on the Hebrides.

As the galley remained a dominant factor respecting both trade and military activities until into the 1600s, the same assumption leads to approximately 1600 as an appropriate end-date.

800 too late a starting date?

800 may well be too late a starting date. The day may come when we will think of Hebridean Galley-Castles as a post-800 sub-set of the Hebridean Sea-Fortifications which began evolving much earlier.

3) LOCATION

Turning from time to space, we need to revise the areas and societies on which to focus and how we describe them, both locally and more globally.

First, each local term needs to be truly local. It needs to focus on the local people and society. In particular it needs to avoid identifying the area as an adjunct of somewhere else. Among other things this helps counter modern thought-patterns in which islands are always remote and peripheral while mainlands are always central. (A strange phenomenon indeed among an island people like the British.)

Second, most if not all Hebridean castles of this period are sea-castles and need to be located in sea-oriented rather than in land-oriented terms.

Third, the descriptive terms need to reflect principal lines of commerce, communication, culture, and military and political life as accurately as possible. Or put negatively it is vital that descriptive terms do not work as barriers to exploring all possible influences on the development of Hebridean castles.

To achieve these goals I believe the best term for the local area is *Hebrides and Hebridean-Mainland*. This is instead of such terms as *Highlands* or *Highlands and islands* or *West Highlands and Islands*, or worst of all, *Outer islands*, all of which imprint the label *Scottish* on the area. Not only do all of them encourage Scottish Diffusionism, they are also anachronistic throughout much of the pertinent 800 year period. *Sudreys* and *Sudreyan-Mainland*, although better than *Hebrides and Hebridean-Mainland* for earlier periods, also would suffer from anachronism for later periods.

An optimum term for the more global area of which the Hebrides and Hebridean-Mainland form a part is *Norse-Celtic Seaways*. These are the seaways stretching from Norway to the Nordreys – now called Orkney & Shetland – with their adjacent-shores of Caithness and Sutherland, through the Sudreys and their adjacent-shores, the Clyde and Galloway, the Isle of Man, the northwestern coasts of modern England, Wales, the southwestern coasts of modern England, and all the coasts of Ireland.

Throughout at least 60% of the period from 800 to 1600 the *term Norse-Celtic Seaways* most accurately reflects the overall historical situation in the Hebrides and Hebridean-Mainland. In important respects this continued to be true until at least the end of that period. One of those respects is the Hebridean Galley-Castle.

CONCLUSION KISIMUL CASTLE: AN ILLUSTRATIVE CASE

In this paper, the historiography of Kisimul Castle has been used to exemplify a number of specific failings of current historiography of Hebridean Galley-Castles. These have included assumptions of Hebridean backwardness, ignoring possible indigenous input, misuse of charter evidence, misuse of Fordun, and ignoring related Shadow-Castles. Each specific instance has, however, been part of broader patterns. These are failures to verify debatable assumptions, ignoring of context, and absence of sufficiently comprehensive studies to justify conclusions reached, violations respectively of the first three propositions of this paper.

The historiography of Kisimul also exemplifies the fourth proposition: the need to replace present prevailing frames of reference with more historically sound approaches. Not even the most tentative conclusions respecting Kisimul's origins can properly be reached without giving full consideration to galleys, inside a contextual time-frame of $c800 – c1600$, and its location in Norse-Celtic Seaways.

Finally, Kisimul is an outstanding victim of the vice of unjustified over-certainty concerning origins. Examples range from Robert Lister Macneil of Barra's firm dating about 1030 to W. Mackay Mackenzie's and John Dunbar's confident dates of no earlier than the second quarter of the 15th century. All three were equally confident that it was built by Macneils, which is certainly only possibly the case.

Indeed *possibly* is the most we can properly say about almost any aspect of the origins of Kisimul Castle. The one clear exception is that we can say that Kisimul was unquestionably a Hebridean Galley-Castle located centrally on the Norse-Celtic Seaways.

Acknowledgements
The ideas in this paper were first presented, thanks to the kindness of Dr. Finlayson, in a talk to the Scottish Society for Northern Studies conference in Barra in April 2002. The ideas themselves could never have come into being had it not been for countless scholars – past and present, professional and amateur – who have given Scotland a golden mountain of detailed archaeological, architectural, and historical information about our built heritage. I stand in deeply appreciative awe of the work they have done.

The April 2002 talk was prepared before I had any detailed knowledge of Historic Scotland's studies of Kisimul made in connection with its lease of the castle. The inclusion of Sally Fosters paper 'Kisimul Castle: recent work by Historic Scotland' in this volume, however, offers readers an opportunity to decide for themselves the extent to which the practices criticised in my paper do or do not continue to dominate current scholarship.

References

Bower, Walter, 1993, *Scotichronicon*, Watt, D E R, (gen'l ed.), Macqueen, John, & Macqueen, Winifred, (eds), vol. 1. Aberdeen.
Cruden, Stewart, 1960, *The Scottish Castle*. Edinburgh.
Dunbar, J, 1978, 'Kisimul Castle, Isle of Barra,' *Glasgow Archaeological Journal*, 5:25-43.
Fordun, Johannis de, Skene, William F, (ed.), 1871 & 1872, *Chronica Gentis Scotorum*. Edinburgh.
McDonald, R Andrew, 1997, *The Kingdom of the Isles, Scotland's Western Seaboard c.1100 – c.1336.*
Mackenzie, W Mackay, 1927, *The Scottish Medieval Castle*. London.
Munro, J & R W , 1986, *Acts of the Lords of the Isles, 1336-1493*. Edinburgh.
RCAHMS, 1971-92, *Inventory of Argyll,* vols. 1-7. Glasgow.
RCAHMS, 1928, *Inventory of The Outer Hebrides, Skye and the Small Isles*. Edinburgh.
RCAHMS, 1946, *Inventory of Orkney & Shetland*, vols.1-3. Edinburgh.
Turner, D J, & Dunbar, J, 1969/70, 'Breachacha Castle, Coll: Excavations and Field Survey, 1965-68,' *Proceedings Society of Antiquaries (Scotland)*, 102.

Kisimul Castle:
Recent Work by Historic Scotland

Sally Foster

THE aim of what follows is to provide an introduction to Kisimul Castle, describing the work that Historic Scotland has undertaken to date. I will flag up what I think are the some of the Castle's more curious and interesting features. But you will soon appreciate that Kisimul still holds many of its secrets and we do not have all the answers to give.

Kisimul Castle is one of the most spectacularly sited castles in Scotland, lying on an island in Castle Bay, Barra. It is also the best-preserved upstanding castle in the Western Isles. It is the residence of a small lordship forming part of the historically significant and geographically distinctive Lordship of the Isles. As such it is an icon of Gaeldom, a highly recognisable survival of a time when Gaelic military power, culture and language held absolute sway over the West Highlands and Islands.

Since 31 March 2000, the Castle has been leased to Historic Scotland by the Macneil of Barra for up to 1000 years. Historic Scotland's efforts since this time have focused on developing a package of management proposals for the most effective protection, conservation, presentation, interpretation and management of the monument. At the time of writing (Dec. 2002), these proposals are shortly to be presented to Macneil of Barra, so that the future of the monument can be decided. The foundation of any Monument Management Plan is knowledge and understanding of the site in question, and this paper will be concentrating on what we have recently learnt about the history and development of the Castle. Equally important will be the key questions that remain unanswered.

This paper describes the outcome of detailed buildings survey, documentary research and preliminary archaeological explorations ably undertaken for Historic Scotland by Headland Archaeology Ltd (Boardman and Brann 2001; Brann, McNeill and Morrison 2001; McNeill 2001; Morrison 2001; Walker and Holden 2001). The overall project was managed for Headland by Dr Tim Holden. In relaying key observations and ideas I am *not* going to cover the detailed survey of the condition of the monument that has also been undertaken by surveyors, architects and structural engineers, a vital and very important strand of our work, managed by Historic Scotland District Architect, Mike Pendery.

Background

Most of what was known about the Castle before the recent research is to be found summarised in two publications. Firstly, the architectural survey and historical review undertaken by John Dunbar of the Royal Commission on the Ancient and Historical Monuments of Scotland in 1967 and 1968 (Dunbar 1978). Secondly, *Castle in the Sea*, R L Macneil's account of his 20th-century crusade to purchase and restore the Castle (Macneil 1964). The Castle has been much altered in the 20th century and it is important to recognise and understand the consequences of this.

Documentary sources for the castle are few. Interesting, if not historically reliable, local traditions prevail, notably regarding early clan history. The surviving documentary evidence strongly suggests that the castle is a late medieval construction, dateable to the period c. 1370 to 1549 and perhaps as late as 1427 to 1549 (Dunbar 1978; Boardman and Brann 2001). The building of the castle may well have been prompted by changes in the structure of political lordship in the region at this time, notably the rise of the Barra-based MacNeill kindred to a new level of political and social influence and independence at the time of the break-up of the wider Lordship of Garmoran. There is no evidence to support or disprove the idea that the MacNeills were resident on the island before the beginning of the 15th century. The absence of any mention in Fordoun's later 14th-century list of island strongholds is likely to be significant and a date of construction in the first half of the 15th century is entirely possible on historical grounds. (For an alternative view, see Macneil, this volume.) Superiority over Barra and Kisimul was claimed by the MacDonald Lords of the Isles (to 1493), directly owned by the crown between 1493 and 1621, by the MacKenzie Lords of Tarbat (between 1621 and at least 1656) and thereafter, apparently, by the MacDonalds of Sleat. However, throughout this period the island and castle were actually under the control of the MacNeills, who abandoned it as their residence in the early 18th century.

The first reference to the castle is in 1549, when Dean Monro described it as 'ane castell in ane ile, upon ane strenthie craig callit Keselum perteining to Mcneill of Barra' (Munro 1961). The MacNeills were descended from Gill-Adhamnain MacNeill, who had received possession of Barra by a charter of Alexander Macdonald, Lord of the Isles, on 23 June 1427. By 15th-century tradition, if not earlier, the MacNeills claimed Irish descent from Niall of the Nine Hostages, although this genealogy is suspect. They were part of an elite group of smaller lairds who were members of the Council of the Isles, the body advising the Lord of the Isles (traditionally meeting on the Council Isle at Finlaggan, Islay). Otherwise very little is known of their medieval history.

The castle was evidently still well defended in the late 17th century. In around 1695, Martin Martin was refused access, reporting: 'There is a stone wall round it two stories high, reaching the sea, and within the wall there is an old tower and an hall, with other houses about it. There is a little magazine in the tower, to which no stranger has access' (Martin Martin 1934, 157).

By the mid-18th century the castle had been abandoned, and in 1795 its roofs and floors may have been destroyed by fire, although in 1816 it is described as 'still tolerably entire'. In 1868 it was rented out as a herring curing station, and this led to the removal of parts of the site for ballast.

The MacNeills finally lost Barra in 1836-7, but chief of Clan MacNeill, R L Macneil, father of the present Clan Chief, Ian R Macneil of Barra, purchased the estate in 1937. The castle lay in ruins until this point. Macneil cleared the site of rubble, and between 1956 and his death in 1970, most of the castle was consolidated and recreated (the kitchen was finished shortly after this) (figure 1).

Description: overview

The aim in what follows is to provide an overview, before touring the castle as it appeared before and after its recreation.[1]

The monument takes the form of an enclosure castle with tower-house, hall and ancillary buildings. Available architectural, documentary and

---

1   This was conjectural and involved the introduction of new material, hence the use of 'reconstruction' under the strict definitions of international charters is not appropriate.

Figure 1. Kisimul Castle in 2000: the interior courtyard.
From left to right, the visible buildings are tower, Tanist House, hall and chapel.
Crown copyright reproduced courtesy of Historic Scotland.

archaeological evidence, both negative and positive, support the conclusion that it was founded in the 1400s. There are those who think the upstanding structures are earlier – Cruden (1960, 42) considered the castle to date from the 13th century, if not earlier – but there is no evidence from the recent work to suggest that this is the case. Reliable diagnostic architectural features are conspicuous by their absence. A lancet loop incorporated in the wall core in the original parapet of the tower gives a *terminus post quem* of the early 13th century for the construction of the tower as the primary building. The medieval remains of the castle reflect the more simple architecture of this area of Scotland. Although there is nothing intrinsically distinguished or special about its architecture, there are few immediate parallels for the precise layout of the castle.

Comparison with other sites, and in particular Breachacha Castle, Isle of Coll, supports the conclusion that Kisimul was founded in the 1400s. Potential parallels with the unexcavated site of Calvay, off North Uist, merit further investigation. With the exception of prehistoric finds there is as yet there is no conclusive evidence for pre-15th century occupation on the island. Whatever the date of the visible upstanding remains, however, it is possible that the rock upon which it stands had been fortified in earlier times. Further archaeological work is the only means of addressing the question of the castle's date and development.

Headland's suggested phasing of the development of the Castle is broadly similar to that of the Royal Commission (figure 2). The terminology used here to describe each building is that adopted by Macneil (1964) and adapted by the Royal Commission (Dunbar 1978). The function ascribed to some of the buildings is questionable.

Phase 1
- *15th century:* construction of tower-house, curtain-wall (later than tower, but conceived as part of same scheme), prison tower and hall; probably other buildings.
- Chapel added, not necessarily long after prison tower.
- Building on site of Tanist House in *15th or early 16th century.*

Phase 2
- *16th century:* tower-house and curtain walls raised; castle entrance narrowed; earliest phase of Gokman's House; crew house constructed.

Phase 3
- *17th century:* Gokman's house extended; castle entrance moved closer to tower-house; conversion of hall into a two storey building; construction of addition; postern gate blocked.

Phase 4
- 20th century recreation and consolidation.

The three-storey **tower house**, standing at the S end, was the first element of the castle to be built, as can be seen from the butt joint between it and the curtain wall, but the curtain wall and tower were surely planned as a single entity from the start (figure 3). (None the less, there are some that dispute the tower's primacy). The tower rises three storeys high. Approached from a stone forestair,

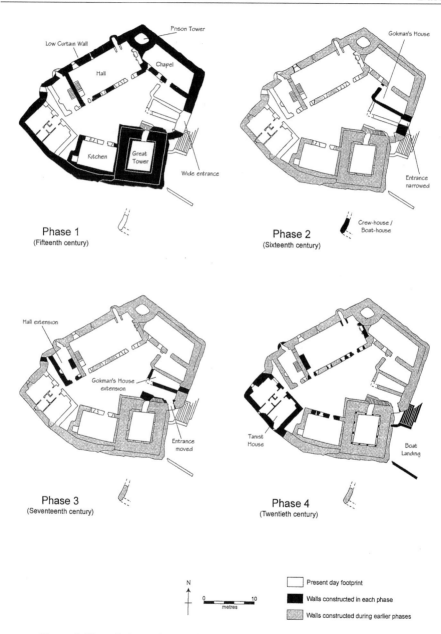

Figure 2. Phased plans of Kisimul Castle (Brann, McNeill and Morrison 2001). Crown copyright reproduced courtesy of Historic Scotland.

Figure 3. Kisimul Castle in 1956: exterior from south, showing joint between tower and curtain wall. The gap in the curtain wall to the left is where the Tanist House now stands. The gables beyond belong to the hall and its addition. Crown copyright reproduced courtesy of Historic Scotland.

a ground floor-chamber is entered from a low doorway and would have provided secure storage space. A small item of gold filigree, provisionally dated to the 16th century, was excavated recently from the floor of this tower – see below. The external staircase continued in timber and/or stone up to the adjacent curtain wall-walk, from which another timber stair, cantilevered from the face of the tower, can be presumed to have given access to the main door, 5.5m above ground level. Inside, a mural stair led from here up to the second floor (the private apartment of the lord) and down to the first (likely to have been the private apartment of a senior, trusted retainer who controlled access to the stores below). All the floors were originally of timber, as was the roof. However, in the 1956-70 recreation concrete floors were cast in situ at first-floor level. The first and second floors were evidently domestic in purpose, both being well lit and having latrine closets within their walls. Both apparently also had timber galleries at their N ends, that above the second floor being in effect within the garret. This was probably where the lord slept. From the second floor, another mural stair leads from the right-hand side of the N window up to the wall-head.

The crenellated parapet encloses a latrine in the SW corner, and shows signs of later heightening. This and other later work included a **box-machicolation** projecting directly above the tower's entrance. On the S and E a timber wall-walk was carried on beams which ran through the parapet; this *may* have supported projecting **external timber hoarding**, designed to protect the tower's exposed outer faces (see below).

The **curtain-wall** that abuts the tower was built later, though possibly by not very much (again, some dispute this). Its parapet, like that of the tower, was also subsequently heightened and provided with a timber wall-walk (possibly also with projecting hoarding) and with a **slot-machicolation** above the wide entrance-gateway. The precise nature of the original gateway is unknown; it may have had a portcullis, but this scenario supposes a substantial timber gate-work behind it, for which there is as yet no evidence. Against one wall stood the so-called **hall**, the development of which is poorly understood. After the tower, this is the most important building in the castle, and it may have had a timber predecessor. Built after the hall, the obtuse angle of the enclosure was occupied by a rounded internal tower, standing apparently no higher than the wall and containing a pit-**prison** with latrine below a guard room. Another building now roofed in timber which is of questionable historical authenticity, lies against the curtain-wall and post-dates the prison tower. It now serves as a mortuary **chapel**, which is what R L Macneil thought it was. The evidence that it was originally one is flimsy; indeed an 1868 reference suggests that the chapel was originally where the so-called Tanist House now stands (Campbell 1998, 209; Boardman and Brann 2001).

Sometime during the 17th century pressure of space led to the postern-gate being blocked up and an addition (extension) being built on the hall, partly blocking the well. R L Macneil called this 'Marion's Addition' in the belief that it could be attributed to the 15th-century 'Marion of the Heads'. A second storey was added to the hall; the tower-house may no longer have been the main lordly residence. The modern buildings bear the closest resemblance to the buildings of this phase. When the hall was recreated in 1958-60, the wall facing the courtyard was largely rebuilt and a concrete upper floor inserted inside. New stone steps to a small balcony were built at one end of the hall, from where access was also created to the addition. Above the hall the floor was divided by Macneil into three rooms by reinforced concrete walls, accessed from a covered corridor in the position of the wall walk.

The other buildings constructed against the inside face of the curtain wall appear to be of a later period. They include a **kitchen** range of two storeys adjoining the tower, now re-roofed. This originally had two ground floor entrances as well as a first floor doorway. In the west corner, the building known as the **Tanist** (or heir's) **House**, rebuilt in 1956-7 from the foundations of what may have been the chapel, was inhabited seasonally until recently. Beside the entrance gate are the unrestored foundations of what R L Macneil described as the **Gokman's** (or watchman's) **House**, the construction of which required the partial closure of the original entrance-gateway.

When the Gokman's house was extended it was necessary to block the entrance-gateway totally and to open a new entrance (the present one). At some point a two storey building now known as the **crew-house** was built outside the castle walls, perhaps to provide additional accommodation.

Description: tour

The following seeks to give you an impression of what the castle looked like before it was consolidated and recreated by Macneil. It has to be acknowledged that the scale, extent and nature of the 20th-century works has affected the monument in terms of our ability to appreciate it as a medieval castle. The concrete, which is decaying badly, has also left the managers of the monument with difficult issues to resolve when it comes to the question of how best to conserve and present the historic fabric of the monument.

In wishing to make the Castle habitable and usable as a clan centre, R L Macneil had to make certain compromises (Macneil 1964, 177):

> In my work I have tried to restore meticulously. At the same time I have endeavoured to make the castle habitable, as we would regard that word in the

twentieth century, and also to secure the utmost durability for future centuries.
Thus I have used reinforced concrete floors and beams instead of combustible
timber ones, such as existed previously. I have used slate roofs instead of thatch.
Then, too, I have tried to consider what modernisation would have taken place if
my family had continued to live in the castle after 1748.

As a medieval building, the tower has fared best through this, but the 20th-
century works have compromised the appearance and historical integrity of the
hall, chapel, prison, tower and kitchen. On the plus side, this build certainly
conveys a sense of the busy, domestic occupation of the castle, something that
is missing from so many ruins (see figure 1).

Unfortunately no detailed building survey existed of the Castle prior to
Macneil's works – the RCAHMS had only prepared a ground plan in 1928
(RCAHMS 1928, 126-8, no. 439) – and we are largely reliant on photographs
for evidence of its appearance prior to its consolidation, etc. These photographs
are of particular value when it comes to the question of what the original form
and development of the wall-heads might have been, notably the question of
whether or not Kisimul had external timber hourdings projecting from both the
tower and curtain wall.

We believe that the walls of the tower and curtain wall were both raised
in close succession, probably in the 16th century. This closely parallels
development at Breachacha on Coll, which also has similar stone box-
machiolations. Some of the evidence for this is now lost under Macneil's
concrete render and it can be difficult to recognise what is what on site, not least
since the modern wall-walk is largely at ahistoric levels.

The easiest way for visitors to appreciate this is by looking at the outside
of the walls, because there are two very obvious lines of holes (figure 4). The
lower line relates to the primary stone wall-walk – they are the weep holes for
this. Those above relate to a secondary timber wall-walk, which rested on the
lower one – they are the putlog holes for the timbers. This is most obvious on
the outside of the hall. You can also see in this figure a change in the external
render, where the wall was heightened, a detail that is now lost. Some of the
crenelles from the first phase of walling were adapted in the second phase, i.e.
they were left as openings of some description.

It has been argued, in the case of the tower-house, that these openings
were designed to allow access to timber hourdings that projected from the upper
wall (figure 5). Headland's analysis of the building has brought out the fact that

Figure 4. Kisimul Castle in 1956: exterior from the northeast. The wall to the right of the prison tower shows evidence for heightening of the wall, details now largely lost under concrete render. Crown copyright reproduced courtesy of Historic Scotland.

Figure 5. Kisimul Castle in 1956: exterior from southeast. Crown copyright reproduced courtesy of Historic Scotland.

access to this parapet could only have ever been through the lord's private chambers (Brann, McNeill and Morrison 2001). As such it is doubtful that its aim was primarily defensive: its value as a recreational facility offering a good view would have also been important to a lord. Either way, in comparison to other castles which are known to have had hourdings, the evidence at Kisimul is rather weak, and certainly seems highly unlikely for any part of the curtain wall.

The curtain wall of the Castle did not all survive into the 20th century, with much of the evidence for the precise form of the wall-heads missing, as well as a very large section of the curtain wall. Little more than part of a gable wall survived of what is now recreated as the Tanist House (see figure 3).

Whilst the so-called addition survived to gable height, scarcely any of the hall did. Figure 6 shows the upper line of holes for the secondary timber walkway. This also gives you an impression of how much of the wall-head above the walkway must also have been lost. You will also note here the vast pile of stones. Macneil undertook extensive stone clearance of the structures, as well as a lot of ground disturbance. When we came to the Castle in 2000, Historic Scotland was not sure whether any significant archaeological levels would remain undisturbed.

Figure 6. Kisimul Castle in 1956: addition and hall during clearance by R L Macneil.
Crown copyright reproduced courtesy of Historic Scotland.

Figure 7. Kisimul Castle in 1956: northeast corner of hall and upper level of prison tower.
Crown copyright reproduced courtesy of Historic Scotland.

Something else to be aware of if you visit the Castle is that we do not know whether Macneil's concrete ground floors relate to a historical floor level. The only way of telling would be to remove the concrete and excavate beneath. Cores taken by engineers for Historic Scotland were examined by the archaeologists and would suggest that further archaeological levels do indeed survive beneath. Note the low doorway on the left of figure 7. This leads from the hall down to a latrine that is flushed by the sea, but was this always quite so subterranean? There is no evidence for a fireplace in this end of the hall, although Macneil created one. A stone basin also sits in the hall in this photograph. Macneil interpreted this as a font and placed it in the building he used as a chapel. It is probably a stone mortar of some description.

In figure 8 you are looking at the prison tower from the opposite side, the chapel end. The chronological relationship of these three buildings is nigh on impossible to disentangle from the remains in their present form, but future

Figure 8. Kisimul Castle in 1956: interior of chapel and upper level of prison tower. Crown copyright reproduced courtesy of Historic Scotland.

archaeology may hold the answers. Note again here the remnants of the stone walk-way and the line of holes for its timber successor above. In the corner, on the right, there must have been a further raised structure of some description.

Next door to the chapel was the original entrance to the Castle. This can be seen most clearly on the outside curtain wall, where its later blocking stands out in the different renders (see figure 5).

This is the point at which to introduce the archaeological excavations which took place in 2001. As mentioned previously, Historic Scotland could not be sure whether any significant sub-surface archaeology had survived the works by R L Macneil. We know from his descriptions in *Castle in the Sea* that he disturbed archaeological levels and made finds that included pottery and a length of gold chain (Macneil 1964, 50-51, 163). Although some of this now survives it is unstratified and of limited archaeological value. Headland Archaeology Ltd undertook a series of small exploratory excavations (figure 9). The aim was primarily to give us an assessment of what might survive, particularly in areas that seemed to us to be of particular interest, and this included the gateway and area of the so-called Gokman's House, of which foundations only survive – marked here as 'remnant wall'. The excavations in Trench 2 were only of a superficial nature, but sufficient to demonstrate that there is a depth of good stratigraphy surviving in this area, and that the Gokman's House was used for metalworking at a late stage in its history. Whether this building was ever built to provide accommodation for a watchman is questionable. This was the only trench that provided evidence of floor surfaces relating to the occupation of the Castle. We can therefore hope that some evidence might perhaps also survive for any internal structures associated with the various phases of entranceway.

If the original wide entrance included a portcullis then a platform would be required for winding gear and counter-weights, and an entrance tower housing these might be speculated. There is slot over the original entrance. Its width indicates that it relates to the narrowing of the entrance and is a machiolation rather than portcullis slot.

Inside the tower, potentially complex stratigraphy still survives to a depth of over 1m. This is part water-logged, which means that there is the potential for recovery of organic remains. The most significant find from 2001, and the one that has caught the public imagination, to judge from media interest, is a tiny, decorated, filigree gold tag, less than 2 cm long (figure 10) (AOC Archaeology Group 2001). This was found in one of two small trenches in the tower-house.

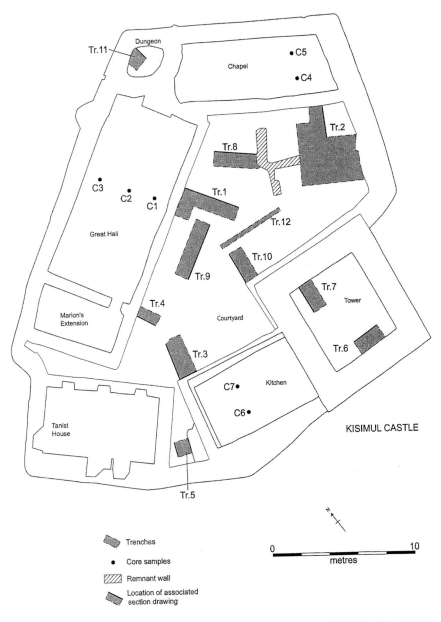

Figure 9. Kisimul Castle: location of exploratory excavations in 2001 (Morrison 2001). Crown copyright reproduced courtesy of Historic Scotland.

Yet to be studied in any detail, it is provisionally dated to around the 16th century and may be of West Highland or Irish manufacture. It seems most likely to have been attached to an object such as a purse, rather than clothing. A further significant find from the tower, but one that is definitely far earlier, is a very nice, worked, burnt flint blade. Knives such as these are most frequently found with male burials of the later Neolithic and early Bronze Age. No evidence for burial was found here, but the possibility is that this and the other flaked stones we found relate to something that was disturbed at the time of construction of the Castle, or that these were curios brought to the site in medieval or post-medieval times.

Elsewhere the trenches provided evidence for a series of levelling deposits associated with phases of building on the island. These confirmed, as we had thought, that the kitchen belonged late in the overall building sequence. In Trench 1 (see figure 9) a stone-built capped drain was found underlying, and hence pre-dating, the wall of the hall. It may prove to be significant that none of the imported wheel-made medieval pottery found so far in any of the trenches

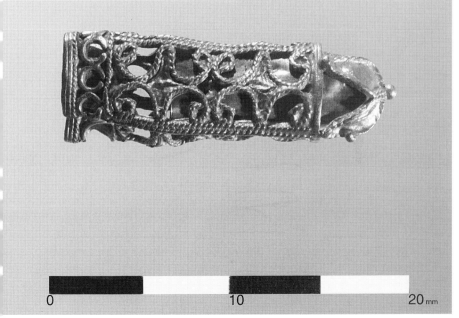

Figure 10. Filigree gold tag (less than 2 cm long) from 2001 excavations at Kisimul Castle (AOC Archaeology Group 2001). Crown copyright reproduced courtesy of Historic Scotland.

pre-dates the 15th century. However, it has to be acknowledged that the 'coarse' hand-made medieval pottery of the Western Isles is little understood, largely because of a lack of well-excavated and securely dated material, so perhaps some of this is earlier. We looked for, but failed to find a second well that Macneil shows as being in the courtyard. No evidence was found in any of the trenches for roof coverings, and we assume that all buildings were originally thatched or shingled. The roofs would have been too steep for the use of turf. Tie-stones for securing the thatch to the hall roof can still be seen.

Beneath the medieval levels was extensive evidence for prehistoric occupation of the island. Pottery, flint and cereal remains are associated with a series of buried soils. The finds suggest a date within the Bronze Age or Neolithic periods. A putative hearth was identified which, together with charred cereal grain, primarily hulled barley with the occasional emmer grain, could indicate a domestic element to the prehistoric settlement. The exact nature and duration of this occupation is, however, unclear at present.

Little has yet been said about what exists outside the curtain walls. Two features are obvious: the crew house mentioned earlier and a tidal fish trap or galley berth. No underwater archaeology survey has been undertaken so it is not known if there is anything else of significance in this area.

Conclusions

So where does this all leave us? We know that the island on which the Castle sits was occupied in prehistory, and that it retains the potential for archaeology to be able to tell us more about its date and development. The most important area in this respect is the gateway, which has the most complicated sequence of construction – at least three successive phases. It would also be nice to know more about the relationship between the hall, prison tower and chapel, the evidence for which is masked by modern works.

On the basis of present evidence, we feel comfortable with the 15th-century date for the visible remains that was suggested by the Royal Commission, although we differ over the interpretation of some features and would place a slightly different emphasis on the development and role of the Castle. We see the tower-house as being a good example of social engineering rather than having a primarily military role. Its interior was divided into two separate lodgings: an inferior first floor was for a trusted official or family member who controlled access to the stores beneath; above were the private chambers of the lord. The small tower-house was not designed to provide public spaces. This interpretation shows the importance of the hall in the original conception of the complex, although we cannot infer anything about the date of the castle complex as a whole from this observation. We can envisage that the lord sat at the west end of the hall, the end which was illuminated by windows on either side. A timber precursor to what survives is a possibility. What we therefore have is the type of image of a medieval lord that might be found elsewhere in Europe at this time, with carefully controlled private and public spaces.

Bibliography

AOC Archaeology Group 2002, *Assessment report on a gold filigree lace end from Kisimul Castle*. Unpublished report for Historic Scotland, arising from work by Headland Archaeology Ltd.

Boardman, S and Brann, M 2001, *Kisimul Castle: the documentary evidence*. Unpublished report by Headland Archaeology Ltd for Historic Scotland.

Brann, M, McNeill, T and Morrison, J 2001, *Report on the building survey of Kisimul Castle, Isle of Barra*. Unpublished report by Headland Archaeology Ltd for Historic Scotland.

Campbell, J L (ed.) 1998, *The Book of Barra*. Stornoway.

Cruden, S 1960, *The Scottish Castle*. Edinburgh.

Dunbar, J G 1978, Kisimul Castle, Isle of Barra. *Glasgow Archaeol J* 5 (1978), 25-43.

Macneil, R L 1964, *Castle in the Sea*. New York (Vantage Press). Reprinted 1975.

McNeill, T 2001, *Kisimul Castle in the context of the Lordship of the Isles and Gaelic Ireland*. Unpublished report for Historic Scotland.

Martin, M 1934, *A Description of the Western Isles of Scotland circa 1695*. Stirling.

Morrison, J 2001, *Archaeological evaluation of the courtyard and other areas within the curtain wall at Kisimul Castle, Isle of Barra*. Unpublished report by Headland Archaeology Ltd for Historic Scotland.

Munro, R W (ed.) 1961, *Monro's Western Isles of Scotland and Genealogies of the Clans*. Edinburgh.

RCAHMS 1928, *Ninth Report with Inventory of Monuments and Constructions in the Outer Hebrides, Skye and the Small Isles*. Edinburgh.

Walker, B and Holden, T 2001, *Kisimul Castle: reconstruction sketches and explanatory notes*. Unpublished report by Headland Archaeology Ltd for Historic Scotland.

Barra and Its History: Through the Eyes and Ears of a Modern *Seanachaidh*[1]

Calum MacNeil

THE reason I am giving this talk tonight is actually because last year, I think it was in April, were the Society for Northern Studies in Barra and there was quite a few speakers travelling with them and I had to do a talk on Barra. Because of this I intend to concentrate mostly on the people of Barra as most of the speakers had specialist subjects. I did it without notes so I have to try and keep to that same kind of talk as I had the last time because they requested it to be recorded and that there be an audience... and that is the reason for the talk tonight. ...

People

I make no apology for speaking mainly about the people of Barra because I feel that wherever you are living in any part of the world it's the people that actually are the most important part of an area. Without people a place really isn't what it ought to be. There are quite a lot of islands in the Western Isles in particular who used to have people living in them and for a variety of reasons they are now abandoned. Latterly it has to do with the fact that the young tended to prefer to live in larger communities and that is quite understandable. The difficulties of isolation that they had to face were fairly overwhelming and because of that they felt they moved on to a bigger town, a bigger place. We had a similar situation with Vatersay until the Causeway went there. We had a steady decline in the population. Eriskay had the same situation. St Kilda was irretrievably lost as was Mingulay, Sandray, Pabbay, and Berneray, Hellisay, Gighay and Flodday in the

---

[1] The following is a transcript from a talk given on Barra in June 2004. Only minimal editing is done to the script in order to retain as much as possible the oral style of the talk. The editors would like to thank Anke Beate Stahl and Ian Macneil for assistance with the transcript.

north of Barra and to a lesser extent in Fuday. These were all populated islands at one time and even in the 1900s, the early part of the 1900s Mingulay, Pabbay and Berneray were still inhabited. The northern islands of Barra at the turn of the century were down to about one shepherd. But prior to that they sustained a reasonable population up to about 112 in case of Hellisay and Gighay. One of the reasons they were populated at that time was because of the pressure on the mainland of Barra as regards land, the scarcity of land and the fact that the population at that time was generally a good one thousand people more than we have now. So you can imagine if you lived in Barra, another one thousand people on the land would be quite difficult to sustain.

Early people

The early history of Barra is mostly – what's written about it anyway – it's quite sparse. The population we have to accept had to move at some point. Mostly they came up from the Iberian coast, from Ireland and from the western mainland of Britain. The Vikings stayed in the islands from the 800s. They left their own impact for the duration that they were here. We have to accept that they inter-married with the local population and the genetic make-up of the people of Barra obviously has that kind of blood in it but they also left an impact on the land. Mostly in names. Very little appears to be left of their buildings, that are clearly identifiable. Sheffield University has done quite a lot of research. They dug quite a lot around, they've had archaeological digs in a very organised manner and they didn't really find a lot of buildings that you would pertain to the Viking presence in Barra. The place-names certainly bear a lot of Viking names especially the coast, the coastal headlands, the bays. The Gaelic inevitably has gone back and you find place-names in Barra which contain Viking and Gaelic with the same name. The Gaelic having been put on top of the Viking name and then you have the Norse and the Gaelic mixed. One example of Vatersay you have a place called Rubha Heilinis. Heilinis is the headland in Norse, whereas Rubha is the headland in Gaelic. So you have the same word twice for the same place. Certainly there are very few places that don't bear Norse names. This is why we find it so difficult to understand why there is so little trace of their houses that they must have lived in.

The Vikings on Barra, it was reputed, had their last stand on the Isle of Fuday after a battle at Bogach na Fala at the North end. The story goes that they were actually – after the battle at Bogach which is at the North end of Barra –

they made their way to Fuday which is off the peninsula of Eoligarry. After a long battle they were tired and they went to sleep and the sentry may also have fallen asleep because it is reputed that the people of Barra had surprised them at night and actually ended up beheading them to the last person and putting their heads in the well which bears to this day the name of Tobar nan Ceann, which is the 'well of the heads'. That was supposed to have been the last Vikings that lived in Barra. Although we have to accept we all bear the same blood.

Coming of the MacNeils

The period between the Vikings and the earliest connection with the charter of the MacNeils. We are only talking about a period of 200 years in which we know the MacNeils definitely had the charter in Barra. They were of course were mainly descended from the MacNeils of Ulster and they're tenacious, they hung on to the island of Barra on and off for that period. And it is fairly certain that they also were in Barra from an earlier stage, pre-Norse, and also during the Norse period. And they may have had their own dealings with the Norse invaders, they may have formed pacts with them but certainly they held on and it wasn't long before they reasserted their dominance.

Individuals

It is from that period that we get to know people as individuals. We of course have heard of Kettil Flatnose and Magnus Barelegs, the main Norse people in Barra, but from the 1400s we know who the MacNeils were, individually they're named and with the MacNeils went their fellow islanders. They were reputed by the 1600s to be sea-farers and pirates, and they also had a quaint way of covering up some other less savoury deeds, they used to go to pilgrimage down to Connaught to Croag Phadruig. It was an annual pilgrimage but MacNeils turned it to good advantage because on the way back they would always take their leave early because the weather was unfavourable as far as they saw it. They were clever enough to know that the western provinces of Ireland would be denuded of population because of the pilgrimage. So they could come along the coast and go into different bays and they could pick up prize cattle - without paying for it. They would come back and they would have quite a lot of cattle to improve the breed that they had here. And the breed of cattle they had here obviously benefitted because they were very much sought after – even up to the present day they are still sought after. But it was a reputed during this period that Granuiale O' Malley was a famous warrior in the south of Ireland had come after MacNeil because she didn't approve of this form of piracy. And it is reputed they had a battle southeast of Barra Head in which according to the Irish the Irish were successful and according to the Barra people they overcame the Irish. What we do know for certain is that Granviale O' Malley went and made her peace with Queen Elizabeth. But the chief of Barra never made his peace with the English queen and when he was taken to court in Edinburgh to face a charge of piracy he went in front of King James, and King James actually looked at him and he was expecting a youngish rogue of a man and he saw a grey haired man who was elderly, very elderly. And he couldn't quite get his head round as to why this was supposed to be a reputed pirate. MacNeil's reply to King James was that he didn't see it as a form of piracy, all he was doing was taking revenge on the queen's ships in view of she was actually responsible for beheading his mother. So King James actually discharged him and told one of his lesser people to take him back to Barra not to have him bothered again. So he was fairly adept at getting out of tight situations.

Introduction

The following history of Barra is fairly standard for what I would say is most of the Western Isles. The only little difference is that the Barra people tended to do a little bit more seafaring and also possibly a little bit more fishing than certainly the islands up to about Lewis. Lewis certainly did a lot of fishing in the north end. But the islands in between didn't quite do as much fishing as they did in Barra. It was during this period that we have records of Barrachs starting to catch fish in reasonable amounts, enough to actually export to Glasgow. They continued exporting that fish right through until the herring came on in the 1870s. It was the mainstay of their income. It formed part of their income even when the kelp boom was on.

Wars and the '45

It would probably be wise now to talk about the MacNeils and Barrachs involvement in the various wars that were fought on the other mainland. They appear to have considered themselves as pirates and engaged in various battles on the mainland. They fought with as much distinction as would be expected of a warrior race. In the '45 they missed the boat, whether by design or whether there was a genuine lack of preparation on their part is not clear. It is reputed that the army was well away on the mainland and underway towards England when the Barra contingent was ready. However, a close scrutiny of records shows there were several Barra people - mostly from Vatersay it has to be said - involved in the '45 and had to pay a heavy price for it including exile and banishment. MacNeil, who was the head of the clan, at the time also suffered because he was involved, if not in the battle, he was involved in a lot of intrigue. That's an inescapable fact and he was shopped by somebody local, he was taken away and imprisoned in Tilbury on the *Pamela*. After doing about 18 months in the *Pamela* he was actually released and taken to shore custody which was a lot more comfortable than the prison ships. It is said that he turned King's evidence. There doesn't appear to be any concrete evidence that this was the case, but whether he did or not, when he got back to Barra, he certainly hadn't changed his ways because when he got back to Barra he was drilling up to 60 men on the west side, in preparation for another uprising. He was again shopped for that, but nothing was done. He was considered a bit too old and nothing would have come of it.

After the '45

It was during this period that we have probably an insight to how he felt. It was apparent that when he was living at the west side of Tangusdale Loch, which is locally known to a lot of people as Loch St Clair, he was living in a place called Lag an Fhliodh which is the `hollow of the chickweed`. He was married to a woman from Harris, a MacLeod, and they had left the castle by this time and he was drilling his men and some say he had become quite disturbed, mentally. Some say he was just drinking too much. And whatever the story is, he would come back at night from drilling his soldiers for a future war and he would be ranting and raving when he crossed the machair in Tangusdale. The wife would take off up the side of the hill, Ben Tangaval, and she would hide behind a boulder high up on the slope. And she would watch him going round in ever-decreasing circles round the house until he flaked out, and then she would come down and he would be quite peaceful then in his sleep. It may well be that the spell on the prison ship maybe unhinged him in some way and certainly wouldn't have been a very pleasant experience for a man getting on in years.

French Canadian war

By 1759, 1758 rather, there was a contingent of Barra soldiers up to about 30 strong went out to fight in the French Canadian war and some did fall at the siege of Louisville. And Lieutenant MacNeil, who was actually the chief's son, gained a commission in the army, the British army. MacNeil wasn't overly keen on this happening, indeed he didn't approve of it at all. However, the son had probably thought he would have to move with times and took this contingent out with him. He was killed at Quebec as well as quite a few of the other Barra soldiers, and indeed when one looks at the records by 1764 only six of the 30 strong contingent were to return back to the island. And when one considers that not many people were killed at Quebec, although it was an important battle, a lot of Barra people proportionately lost their lives there. And certainly it lends credence to the fact that Wolfe always maintained that one of the virtues of the Highland soldiers was that there was no great mischief if they fell. And certainly the Barra people fell out of all proportion to the amount of people who was involved in the battle. It doesn't necessarily mean that all of them actually fell who didn't come back. May well be that some deserted and some of actually just stayed out there.

An insight into the MacNeil's thinking at the time is that they were having games on Borve Machair, and when the news of the son's death came to them by messenger, the messenger asked them if they would cancel the games. MacNeil said "No, the games will proceed, because my son did not honour me in life and I shall not honour him in death!", which meant that he certainly bore a grudge of some sort towards his only son and heir.

Grandson succeeds as chief – American War

Because of the death of Lieutenant MacNeil, the grandfather having died in 1763 at Borve, and the grandson actually took over as chief. He would only be about six or seven at this time and he was put under the care of the MacNeil of Vatersay, a relative and a direct line from the MacNeils of Barra but through the second family who had been usurped in 1610. They actually took over the care of the grandchild of MacNeil and he was brought up with the Vatersay family. He was put through college in Aberdeen and he joined the British army and he also took out a contingent of British soldiers, of Barra soldiers, to fight in the American war. He was also wounded in the arm during that fight and the page and piper that he had was a man called Callum MacNeil, Callum son of John son of Roderick, who were the MacNeils' hereditary pipers. He had been a page with Lieutenant MacNeil when he died and he attended him before he died as well. And when Colonel MacNeil fell wounded in the American war he spent six weeks trying to suck the bullet out of his arm and eventually succeeded and he told MacNeil that he had more of MacNeil's blood, the true MacNeil bloodline, than MacNeil himself had. He advised MacNeil to make his way back for Scotland or his bones would rest in America the same as his father's had. And MacNeil took his advice and came back.

Emigration

The other Barra soldiers who were fighting with MacNeil in the American war were more fortunate. They were offered grants of lands in Nova Scotia. They were known as the Heirlichy Grants. There was a man Timothy Heirlichy, a man of Irish descent, who was fighting for the British Crown. Their grant of land was divided amongst the Barra soldiers and the grants were according to rank. The single Barra soldiers took up the grants, the married ones didn't take the grants of land but they took the pension. And they came back to Barra and after several years they had enough money to decide to emigrate. They emigrated in 1791. Up to 200 Barra people went out to Pictou with view to settling in Nova Scotia but there was also Prince Edward Island.

Now they weren't actually the first organised emigration out of Barra. The first organised emigration from Barra took place in 1771 on a ship called *Alexander* which we hear very little of. There were eight Barra families who made up the Glenalladale emigration mostly of Clanranald MacDonalds but with a few families from Uist pulling out at the last minute the Barra families took up their places.

It is interesting to note why these people are so keen to emigrate. The kelp had been established in Barra by the 1750s or just several years earlier, maybe, but certainly by 1750 the kelp was very well established and it provided a reasonable income although the wringing and drying of the kelp was slave labour. At the height of the kelp boom, a family involved for two to three months in the summer would be expected to cut about 65 ton of wet kelp, take it up onto the shore and when it was dried take the peat down from the hill, fire the kiln, dry it and reduce it down to – that 65 ton would yield about 3 tons of dry – which the landlord MacNeil could sell for up to 22 pounds a ton during the boom. The tenants, the whole family, would be paid 2 pounds for that ton, for that three months of labour. They would be expected to make 6 pounds in ready cash from this kelp every season. It cost about £1.50 for a ton to ship it to Liverpool which wasn't very high, so the profit of the landlord was quite enormous. It wasn't just the profit of the landlord, the fact that the tenants were paid 6 pounds in ready cash means that MacNeil who actually paid them actually knew that they had this money. And this is exactly what he would charge on average for the crofts. They were expected to pay an average of 6 to 7 pounds for per croft even in those days of 1810-1811. This is an average rent. And when one considered that in 1978 they were still paying only 7 pounds on a croft on average it shows you what kind of rack renting was going on and that the landlord had probably shifted his allegiance from kinship to economics.

This was the impetus along with the soldiers' description of Nova Scotia and Cape Breton that made these people emigrate. They were harried at home, they had no security of tenure and a trip across the sea was quite attractive as far as they were concerned especially with the tales that the soldiers had coming back. They described a reasonable land with trees and where they would be free of landlords and that was the most important thing that they wanted to be free of. A detailed look at the immigration to Prince Edward Island will show you what they really though really thought. They were offered 3000 year leases on their land, a tenancy for 3000 years. The rates were very favourable, they certainly weren't extortionate. They increased slightly year on year but certainly nothing in comparison to what they had here and certainly the land was much, much better. But strangely the eight Barra families who went there decided to buy themselves out of that obligation that they had to Glenalladale and the simple tenet that they had was that they didn't leave the old country to be clear of one landlord to go and start a new life in a new country to be beholden to another landlord however benevolent. They wanted to own their own land. That's what they wanted to do. They didn't want to pay rent, they didn't want to be tenants, they wanted to own their land. They wanted independence. And they actually bought themselves out for 40 pounds per family. And they moved further along Prince Edward Island and bought their own land. And considering money wasn't very plentiful and it took them quite a while to do so but it was very important. It was an important principle.

The emigration from Barra went on. In 1802-03 there was about 700-800 people left Barra in several emigrant vessels. There was sporadic emigration between 1806-13, massive emigration again in 1817, and 1821 right through to

1828 and again of a sporadic nature to 1835. And then one last emigration of 70 people in the 1840s. That was the end of the emigration to Prince Edward Island and to Cape Breton as far as Barra was concerned. At that time the blight that had appeared in Barra and Ireland in 1746 had also appeared in Cape Breton and was of equally devastating effect so that Cape Breton was no longer an attraction. What happened to them out there was that land was getting scarce because not only were Barra people emigrating, people from the whole of the Western Isles were emigrating. From all the islands and the whole West Highlands and land was getting scarce to the degree that the front lands, which were the shore lands, averaging about 200 acres would have to go to the head of the family but any grown up member of the family would have to take up the rear lands which were more inaccessible and agriculturally less viable.

Loss of the Estate – Gordon of Cluny

By 1849 things had become quite severe in Barra as far as the people were concerned. MacNeil, the Colonel, had died. His will had tied the General, the successor to the Estate. He had made promises in the will that couldn't be met by the Estate because the money wasn't there. And every beneficiary in that will, nobody would actually accept a lowering of their share. So the successor, who became the General, was left scurrying around looking for more money. The factory which he installed at Northbay was never a success, far from it. It actually bankrupted his estate, and one of the people who was a creditor, Colonel Gordon of Cluny, called in the debt and MacNeil was put to the horn in Edinburgh and eventually Colonel Gordon was successful after several bids in buying Barra. It wasn't all bad from what I could work out. He had plans for the inland in Barra, which didn't amount to very much, and one wonders what he intended to do, but he had plans to turn the inner parts of Barra into fertile land. We would assume that he meant take a lot of sand in and reseed it. These plans fell through and he became on very bad terms with the population. They were starving; he wasn't prepared to feed them, far from it. He was actually selling off the land to sheep-farmers. The population from the west side, which is the most fertile part of the mainland, were trans-shipped to the east side, and the village of Earsary, for example, in 1810 had three tenants sharing two crofts. By the 1850s there was about 28 families living on that land, 28 families. So you can imagine what kind of pressure that land on the east side was under. The fertile land on the west side was by then under one single farmer. The same was true of the north end although most of Kilbarra had already been cleared by the MacNeil of Barra in 1824. The situation was dire as far as Barra was concerned. The landlord Colonel Gordon wouldn't come to Barra, he wouldn't listen to any entreaties that people put to him, he wouldn't listen to any Member of Parliament. He was deaf to all pleadings and his ground officers harried and chased the population that had moved and had no land. They went to the shore where they were able to fish and at night they would pull the boats ashore and overturned them onto turf walls and used the sail as an additional shelter and they would be forced to eat shellfish and whatever fish they could catch in season.

This was still not good enough as far as Gordon was concerned. He had the ground officers and various constables on the island. He ordered them to burn all their boats and that would eventually force them off the island. And this is what happened. Quite a lot of them between 1849 and 1850 made their way to Tobermory, to Inverness, to Edinburgh, to Glasgow, to Nairn, to Dunoon, Inverary, various places. And all of them, they were on the steps of various town halls starving depending on the local population to feed them. The remaining population, 450, were shipped onto a ship called the *Admiral* and this was the last major emigration out of Barra, probably the only one that was actually forced. They joined the *Admiral* at Lochboisdale and they joined another 1500 who had already left from Uist and Benbecula and they went to Quebec. When they arrived in Quebec they were in a sorry state. It was late in the year. It was in September. You can imagine they had no English, very, very few of them could write. Indeed, it is interesting to note that the man who actually signed the petition that we have was a man who had come in from Tiree, a Hector Lamond. He could read and write because he had been taught to read the bible. And he actually signed the petition on their behalf. And they actually just appended their X to it as their mark. And they were left destitute. It has to be said that that wasn't the case while they were aboard the *Admiral* itself. The master's wife was busy all the voyage, sowing up flour bags, and whatever she could lay her hands on, to make clothes for both adults and children. We have to look at the situation when they got to Quebec, they were put in quarantine, and it was commented by one of the customs officers that an adult had passed through his inspection with nothing to wear except a woman's petticoat. And he was a man. You can imagine in what kind of poverty and how destitute these people really were to face the Canadian winter. It is probably the saddest emigration that ever took place out of Barra, and the only real one that was forced. I think for us the saddest part is that we have never been able to trace many of these people. We can trace most of the people that left Barra. There is no difficulty because they kept records in Nova Scotia, Cape Breton, Prince Edward Island. They kept their own genealogy. They know who they are, they can trace their families back and we can trace them. But from 450 people on the *Admiral* we can only identify definitely one family that originated in Sandray and Vatersay. And they settled at Stephen Township in Huron County. And when you consider that a lot of people, a lot of families emigrated from that 450 it is amazing that we haven't been able to pin them down to where they settled. The other way of looking at it is how many of them actually survived. They survived the voyage, probably only half a dozen died on the voyage, but how many survived the Canadian winter? It is a subject where a lot more detailed study is required than has taken place up 'till now.

Recovery – the herring

Putting that period behind it was 30 years before actually Barra could rise off its knees. A full generation would pass before Barra would actually make any kind of mark again. And that came about for a variety of reasons. It takes about 30 years for people who have been brow-beaten and knocked to the ground so many times to actually reassert themselves. The saviour of Barra was the herring fishing. Although they had been involved in white fishing from time immemorial and taken the fish all the way to the Clyde in open boats, they had never really been heavily involved in herring because they didn't have the salt to properly cure it. Now the East coast fishermen had come to Barra certainly from the 1840s, 1841 they were visiting the Barra islands and by the 1870s the herring had taken off west of the Hebrides. By the 1890s it was an interesting situation. This bay would be full of up to 600 herring boats, Vatersay would have probably 300-400 herring boats, all kinds of sheds and jetties from the point of Oronsay all the way around to the Bagh Beag of Castlebay, round from the pier now right to the entrance of the small bay round the back here. Vatersay Bay, the whole of the south side of that bay, was just jetties and curing stations. During this period the Barra population would meet and mingle with people from other islands. They would also mingle with people from the mainland, from Ireland, from the East coast. They would follow the herring all the way down to Lowestoft. And they also had an important feature, they didn't really have much of it before, they were able to go to school. And being able to read and write made a great difference in how they could articulate themselves.

By the 1880s they had done enough agitation to force the authorities to look at the land question in Barra. A Barraman was always a fisherman but he never forgot the land. And by the time of the mid 1880s the demand for land was increasing and the inequities of the previous 50 to 60 years, they were determined to reverse all that. The days of the big farmers to the north end of Barra were literally numbered at that stage. Agitation took place after the crofting act continuously until they succeeded in forcing the sale of Vatersay, and turning it into 58 crofts. They raided the lands at the north end and after the First World War they actually forced the sale of the last part of Eoligarry. And this can be put down to education. They always had the desire to do it but they didn't have the means to do it. By the 1880s onwards they were able to actually argue their own case and they had very, very powerful orators within their own community.

After the First World War the herring boom was over. The markets that they had depended on so heavily in the Baltic, Russia, Germany, the markets had collapsed. There was no sale for the herring. The herring itself was getting scarce and herring boats were lying all round the bay, defunct, weathered and rotting, and people were drifting back into the merchant navy; something which they had been involved in from the 1850s, but not in a really big way. After the War that had all changed. The merchant navy was the mainstay of employment. The herring boats that that they had tended so fondly and fished so well were now being cut up for fence posts. Very few of the old boats survived to be motorised. A few stalwarts remained at the herring and that was the case until the Second World War.

Last major emigration

By 1922-23 was the last major emigration out of Barra, that went to Alberta in Canada. It was an organised emigration, a priest had organised it, Father MacDonell, one of the many priests that have visited Barra's history. The emigration itself left a bad taste in the mouth of a lot of people in Barra. It wasn't a success. The people that went out were reluctant to admit that it wasn't a success. The general trend was that the people that left promised to write to the people who were left behind and that if things went well they would follow them out to Canada in a subsequent emigration. In my own grandfather's case his elder brother left. He was 57 when he left with his family and he never wrote until 1939. It was a long time after he left. By that time my grandfather had decided it wasn't worth going because he himself was getting old now. And the story is that some of them made it in the Prairie with a lot of difficulty and the others just headed for the sea which was Vancouver. And most of them actually settled out in Vancouver. And that was the case with quite a lot of people from Uist as well.

The story about the priest's involvement left, like I say, a sour taste. I recently read an article that I'd had sent from Canada about it. It certainly goes to a fair degree to exonerate him and it possibly isn't an apology for what he did, but it appears that the real reason for the problem was that the emigration was oversubscribed. They had only planned to have so many people going out , and I forget the numbers, but far more people actually chose to emigrate than ought to have gone. If possibly less had gone then more had gone a few year down the line, it might have been more successful. From then onwards Barra actually was dependent mostly on the merchant navy and sheep and cattle. Fishing didn't reassert itself until the 1960s and it's formed a reasonable part of the economy since then.

Where people lived

The other thing I would like to touch on before I finish is the housing and the evidence of where people were in Barra. Sheffield University has done a lot of work over the last 12-13 years in Barra. They have done it sensitively and with permission from the local people and have certainly done a lot of work, very detailed work and they have certainly opened my eyes as to what used to go on. And the places in the hills and moors that we used to tramp as children just showed up as green patches with stones, but they have now identified them, they have dug them, they've shown what was underneath, something that we would never dream of seeing. It was a perfect example of an Atlantic Round House down at Allt Easdail on the road to Vatersay. When I look at that building, the way it's been dug out with its internal divisions and how well it has been put together, and I look at the black house that is actually overlying it and what is now part of the rear half of the black house is left and the other half was over the round house and it has been dug away and removed. There is no comparison to the Black House of the 1800s as far as architecture is concerned. The Round House was superior, so certainly as far as housing was concerned the Barra people in the Round House had probably a far better house than they had in the 1800s. And I can't see any other place in Barra with exception of the new houses, the Manse and MacNeil's Mansion down in Eoligarry and Vatersay

House. Apart from that the Black Houses were really poor in comparison. The rest of it is, where the Black Houses were mainly; but on the hills there was one thing that used to actually make me wonder. There are settlements out on a hill called Ben Tangaval. And all you would find is a row of fairly large houses by our standards but was all huge boulders, foundation boulders. And I often used to wonder, where did the rest of the stones go? Who took them? Were they so desperate to build houses somewhere else that they actually came and moved these top layers of stone completely from the site? And now getting answers as to one of the questions what was going on. It was only when they started digging out at Allt Easdail that they started finding out the truth. They never had any stones in the first place; it was turf walls, and the timbers came from the roof right through the turf walls into the base stones of the foundation. The reason for people doing that is very simple. They were quite warm and why should they build a stone house when at the end of the year if you didn't have the rent you were evicted. You couldn't take the stone with you, you could take the roof which was the thing you couldn't get anywhere else, timbers, but the turf you just kicked into the ground and that was the end of it. So it was really a matter of necessity. They didn't have the security anyhow to be able to build houses, and the reason, probably, they weren't told about it is purely to do with a sense of shame that people felt in the 1950s. They didn't want to admit that people actually lived in turf houses. But if you look at that book, it was actually turf shingle. The turf was laid as you lay stone but on the outer side of the wall the turf was laid on end, all round to shed the water and that woman wasn't ashamed to live there. But people by the 1950s probably didn't think you should be talking about it, admitting that people were so poor. People don't have any difficulty with that now of course, but during that period I would say they certainly did. Certainly, looking at Donald there and myself, when we went to school we had to walk through a village that still contained quite a number of Black Houses as well as what they would call White Houses. They were living there into the 1950s and indeed, in one particular instance, they were living in a house which was into the 1960s and 70s. But you won't find many evidence of the amount of Black Houses that was in this place as they were taken away and put into the roads, especially if they happened to be in a location that was beside the road. They would be used as infill and that's one of the reasons you don't find many ruins. You certainly find ruins out in the moor but you won't find them along the road.

I think we can end now. Is that an hour?

Questions

Q: It seems that your relationship with the landlord is really the source of all of Barra's problems. Other countries in the northern hemisphere don't seem to have had quite the same problems as we have in the northwest of Scotland. What do you think about that?

Calum a'Chal: Well, we certainly can't blame the present landlord. Either the Department of Agriculture, which owns quite a bit of Barra, or the MacNeil. We have to look at the period. It was really after the '45 rebellion when it really starts to implode. They needed the people to fight wars. They needed troops, they needed the men. The chief's importance wasn't as a landlord. He was important as a fighting man, in charge of fighting men.

Q: This is pre '45?

Calum a'Chal: Pre '45. After the '45 they become out and out landlords. They weren't equipped for it, mentally weren't equipped for it and they certainly weren't equipped mentally to be estate managers. Their carry-on down in the fleshpots of London bear ample evidence that they certainly were more concerned about their own welfare than the welfare of their tenants. Now in MacNeil's case, both the Colonel and his son, the General, they were certainly good soldiers and they weren't good estate managers, nor were they very good landlords it has to be said. People make excuses for the Colonel as opposed to his son, the General. But if you look at it fairly, the Colonel also had his own difficult situation. He was involved with the first emigrations, and he encouraged the first emigrations by taking the tacks from the tacksmen, taking the land from them and then applying it to subtentants. Now, most of these tacksmen were from MacNeil lineage – the tacksman of Vatersay, the tacksman of Scurrival, the tacksmen of Grìn, Tangusdale, Breivig, Earsary, Bhaslan – all relatives of the MacNeil one way or another. Some of them quite close relatives. They also employed sub-tenants. Shaw was the only person who wasn't directly related to MacNeil, but he certainly was in Barra for quite a while as a head schoolmaster. And what we have to look at is that when he started to talk about breaking Barra into individual crofts, the tacksman didn't like this and they chose to emigrate and they took most of the tenants with them. But that's not the full story because the tacksmen weren't that much better than the landlord was. And why should you owe any allegiance to the tacksmen? But the conditions overall in Barra meant that emigration was a favourable option as far as people were concerned. They were very, very attached to the island but you can't live as a slave, a virtual slave all your life and that's really what it amounted to.

When the kelp started to fail, he started to move in on the white fish which they were selling to Glasgow. He wanted control of that. With no input whatsoever from him. He just wanted the money.

Q: Pre '45 there must have been a reasonable standard of life.

Calum a'Chal: Reasonable for the whole population of course. The population did not really start to increase on Barra until after the 1760s when the potato took hold, they were better fed, more carbohydrates, they had more energy. The kelp gave them ready money although it became very labour intensive and unhealthy. What you find in the old Parish Records, Baptismal Records, a lot of males died young with a child born after their death and that meant that these people died in the prime of life. Women might survive a wee bit longer and what you find with women is that they generally die if there is twins involved. They didn't normally die in childbirth with one single child. They were robust enough to withstand that kind of rigour every two years. But the men were worn out and they would obviously die with bronchial complaints with the smoke inhalation from the kiln from the kelp. The damp, continuous immersion in water. To cut the kelp, it's not what we think of nowadays, gathering it on the shore, that was no use whatsoever for processing, it was too contaminated with sand. That was only fit for manure on the land. The kelp for manufacturing it had to be cut in the sea. You would cut in one place every three years. You cut it once and you had to leave it fallow for three years, you would have to move on. You had a long sickle and you had to wade up to your shoulders in the water to cut it under water, then you had to float it in, so you were damp, no means of actually drying yourself. You then had to go and wait for the high tide, tie it up in rafts, take it up upon the shore. You had put it in the kiln, dry it first then start getting it ready for the kiln. Barra, especially round this side of Barra, the peat is right up, it's nearly a thousand feet. It's not so bad in the northeast but up at this end of the island it was absolutely terrible to win that amount of peat to fire these amount of houses and then the few clothes you had, still dry, and how could you not end up unhealthy. And obviously this was having an impact on people. They weren't stupid. They would have to realise that it was an unhealthy occupation and they would have to be out of it. And that's the way emigration was so attractive. But after 1803 they introduced the Passenger Acts which meant that they tried to make it as unattractive as possible, as expensive as possible, for people to emigrate and the excuse they were using was that they were forcing these emigrant vessels to improve their accommodation. But really, what the ship owners did once these new regulations came in, they just passed the cost of these improvements onto the fare paying passenger. Which meant that the emigration was beyond their grasp. It was too dear. And that meant that they couldn't emigrate from 1803 until really 1817 before we see the next batch of major emigrants. There were sporadic ones in between, but not many, and the reason was a connivance between the landlords and parliament to pass this act, to make it more expensive to emigrate and to retain people on the land to be used in the kelp industry.

Q: Was there much more land under cultivation in those days?
Calum a'Chal: If there is a low sunset you could look. When the sun sets at Caolas you can see the cultivation ridges clearly marked at Goirtean. The land was heavily cultivated right up as far as physically possible to do so. In Cliad, for example, it is almost right up to the summit of the hill. It is quite a high hill. They had to use every available bit of ground. And of course they had to keep the stock up in the hill away from the crops. They had what was called a grass keeper.

Q: Can you tell us anything about the ship that grounded off Vatersay in 1859?
Calum a'Chal: 1853. The *Annie Jane*.

Q: They started off from Liverpool.
Calum a'Chal: They were from Liverpool. That was their second attempt. The first attempt ended up in disaster. They had to go round the south of Ireland and came back into Liverpool and they had to replace the topmast, restow the cargo. On the second attempt they ended up as far as St. Kilda, again they started to lose some of the topmasts and they were forced to turn back. They were running towards Barra Head. Couldn't get round it. They were forced to turn back and run up along the western shore. Some said that the intention was to find one of the channels, others said that the ship could not be handled anymore. It happened during the equinoctial gales in late September, probably with high tides and very, very difficult sea. They ran on the beach west of Vatersay where that memorial is. They broached to there. Had it happened during the day, had it happened at a different part of the tide they might have been saved. It's just that

circumstances worked against it. By next morning it was virtually flat calm and by that time most of them were drowned.

Q: People on the ship were from up here?

Calum a'Chal: There were allegedly some people from Skye on the original voyage, but they got out of it by the second voyage. They were mostly Irish, from the Lowlands of Scotland, mostly tradesmen on their way to Canada. Quite a lot of tradesmen.

Q: Were there ridges on Greian?

Calum a'Chal: If you look down to Cliad Village and if you look straight up to Beinn Chliaid, near the top you see a small dyke running across. You see the cultivation that is down there. The problem that you find in Barra, I would say, if you look at the amount of arable land alone, is that people must have been really desperate. They grew potatoes, oats, they grew barley. According to some reports in the early 1700s, possibly late 1600s the west side of Barra had a lot more land than there is now. They were talking when they were giving evidence to Dr Walker in the 1760s that the old-timers could remember grazing cattle where there is nothing but seaweed and rocks now. The only places where that would happen are at Seal Bay near Allasdale and possibly past the Isle of Barra Hotel. At low tide you can see that that was one spot. You don't have to go back thousands of years to see it. You only have to go back a few hundred years.

Q: The grass seems rather short. It must have been overgrazed. How many sheep and cattle did a family have?

Calum a'Chal: At that time there were many sheep and a lot of horses. Every household had a horse. In some cases some had three horses. The horses were useful for work. They could have shared a horse, because there wasn't work for a horse every day. And they could have lessened the pressure on the grazing by dispensing with some of the horses and just sharing the rest of them. Certainly that would have changed matters. There would have been more grass for the cattle. Horses are quite heavy grazers. You could see that they didn't work every week of the year.

Q: The grass is very short on the islands just now. Is that the grazing rather than the season?

Calum a'Chal: If you take the sheep or the cattle away it soon grows. I haven't been up to the Barra Head islands recently to see what it is like now.

After so many hundred years they've stopped having stock there. What I find, anyway, is that if you take stock off for a while, the grass just gets dry and you can't use it for anything. See the deserted village of Goirtean just opposite Caolas when you go across the causeway. If you look back, that's a deserted village that was actually cleared. Most of the population went to Beaver Cove in Cape Breton Island in 1822. There was a family of MacKinnons. There were ten children from two wives. There were eight from the first wife and two from the second wife and they were all married prior to leaving Barra with their own families. They all emigrated and most of them still lived in their own village of Goirtean before they left. And it was only the Campbells and a family of MacSweens who left after that. They were cleared by 1833 to make way for a sheep farm.

The whole of Ben Tangaval peninsula, Vatersay and Sandray were cleared for the sheep, to form one sheep farm. One of these places on its own wasn't enough, wasn't practical for the farmer. Vatersay on its own wasn't enough because they needed more grazing. People in Sandray and Vatersay were moved on to Uidh which was a neck of land on Vatersay and they were subsequently cleared in 1851. A few of them actually settled in Gleann. The ones in Bentangaval who didn't emigrate came out to Kentangaval and Nasg and then went to Uidh and then were cleared along with the rest.

But my own family and those related to the MacNeils they didn't fare any better for being closer related to MacNeil. They had a tack of land. Their father, Hector Òg, had a tack of land at Earsary and Seumas, his son, organised along with his brother Eachainn Bàn the emigration with Hugh Dunoon in 1802. Seumas MacNeil came back to organise further emigrations. He made a return voyage and he went to Arisaig to organise a further emigration. He was on very very bad terms with the Colonel, his cousin, that year and so was the priest who was also involved, James A. MacDonell. They both drowned in the Sound of Sleat while organising the emigration. They were shipwrecked. Ruairidh Bàn, my great-great-greatgrandfather, he stayed in Barra. He didn't fare any better than any non-relative. He started off in Kilbar. When two of the sons got married, they moved to Cliaid from Kilbar, ended up in Allasdale and even stayed in Uist for a while. They went to Morghan which is in Northbay, moved on to Bogach, then they went to Fuiay, which is a small island, along with another four tenants, when the factory was in business. My great-great-grandfather Alasdair was cleared from there and came to Brevig. Then they went to Gleann and finally to Kentangaval where he died. His brother, Iain Donn, went the same way, although he had one voyage less, he moved from Brevig to Buaile nam Bodach where he died. One was 94, the other one was 95 when they died. There is a physical description of them in a book called *The Lay of Deirdre* by Alexander Carmichael.

Q: Was the movement of population exceptional or typical?

Calum a'Chal: Very typical. Strangely enough, there must have been a few crawlers amongst them. We find some families who stayed on. It makes you wonder what they did. All the rest appear to be completely mobile. They seemed to be very unsettled. They were chucked from one place to another. But you see the odd family that is stuck in one place.

Q: Did any ever come back to Barra from the New World?

Calum a'Chal: Yes. I only know one definite man called Ruariridh Ùr MacIntyre, the son of Allan MacIntyre. The ones that went out first across went as pioneers. Twenty years down the line they tended to kind of maybe look down on the newcomers. The newcomers weren't quite as good as the old settlers, as far as they were concerned. Ruairidh Ùr MacIntyre came back. It is a strange story, and it's a true story what happened. On the way out to Nova Scotia they had a French-Canadian crew and they experienced the same problems similar to what they had on the Annie Jane. Ruairidh Ùr was forced to join the crew and go up the mast to save the ship. The skipper thought so highly of him that when they got to Nova Scotia he asked him if he would make the return journey with him and he would take him and any of his relatives out free of charge and the return voyage again. They were coming back with timber and going out with emigrants again. This is what he did. He took his mother out with him. I find it difficult to understand, because she had children here. Her eldest daughter was married to a man called Mìcheil Mòr MacDonald who had Uist connections. They went out in 1817, so certainly could have gone out to see her own daughter. But she left two daughters here, one of them was my own ancestor, and she left another son here. So why did she go? It's quite strange what actually happened. I could understand it if she had no family left in Barra. She went with him and that was it. Maybe he was the blue-eyed one.

Q: Do you get many visitors from Canada?

Calum a'Chal: Yes we do. The descendants certainly come back. There is another strange story. I can't vouch for its veracity but there is a ring of truth in it. There was a woman who went to Canada, a MacKenzie. There was only one family called MacKenzie on Barra with several families all from the one ancestor. The MacNeil had a brother who – the story goes – wasn't all there. He was wandering around from village to village. And he had this bag with him. One day he called on this woman who offered him whatever she had to eat and she sat him down because she knew him. And she asked him: "What have you got in that bag?" He answered: "I've got my money in it. I've got gold in it and I'm going to bury it." She first thought nothing of it because she knew he wasn't quite sensible. He went away round the headland and then came back without the bag of gold. And she found it strange, and wondered whether he actually did what he was saying he was going to do. There was a man called Carmichael who didn't belong to Barra who got wind of this story in Cape Breton one night at a ceilidh with the woman's husband. And he wanted MacKenzie to come with him Barra to find the gold. All the way from Cape Breton. But MacKenzie's wife wouldn't hear it. The only condition that she would let him go was if he took her with him. But he didn't have the money to pay for the two fares. He only had enough money to pay for himself and Carmichael to come back. So Carmichael went to Barra without him. The strange thing was that although he wasn't connected to Barra – had no connections at all to Barra – when he went back to Nova Scotia to Cape Breton he went back to the village, he upped sticks and bought a big plot of land in a desirable area. He settled there on a big farm. But nobody could explain where he got the money from. And then they started to believe it was true, that he had actually found the gold. They couldn't figure out any other way he could have got the money. They knew he'd come back. As I know the village, the two villages that woman was in – before she left she was living in Kentangaval – and then they moved to Tobhta Driseach which is just the lower part of Gleann. They emigrated from there in 1821. If MacNeil had passed this village there is only one place that he could have put the gold in. He put the gold in a crevice round a point of land. And Carmichael had asked the man: "Do you know this point of land?" And he said: "Yes, I know exactly where it is." And he said: "That's where the gold is." There is a small cleft in the point over by this cliff. And there is of course the Cave of Gold at the back of Garrygall which is another place where you've got a crevice going into the rock. These are the only places where he could possibly have put it. I've checked it out already. It is not lying on top of the ground. I don't know exactly if that actually ever happened but it is certainly a story in Cape Breton.

Q: What is the main occupation in Barra today? What do people do?

Calum a'Chal: There is the council which employs all the people to the schools, to the hospital and the health board. You've got a fish factory. You've got the hotel. You've got the fishing industry in various forms and the building trade. And you've got the merchant navy, not quite what it used to be but still of significant amount.

Q: Anybody doing crafts?

Calum a'Chal: Well, at the moment there is a craft shop down in Skallary. The owner does paintings and various crafts and you've got the Toffee Shop which is down here. That's another small business. We have Margaret Somerville at the north end who is a sculptor and does quite a bit of work.

Q: Crofting?

Calum a'Chal: There is less crofting on a communal basis. When I came back to live in Barra in 1978 crofting was more active. I think the biggest problem with crofting is paper, the same as happens in the industry I am now in – fishing. Every day there is a letter that comes through, a catalogue comes through, somebody wanting information. And that's quite disappointing for the economy. I think that successive governments for 20 odd years have gone in and out and been producing bureaucracy.

Q: I have another question. I was reading an article about the storytelling capacity, the old tradition in Barra and how some families have what they might call a *seanachaidh*. A *seanachaidh*, a storyteller with a memory. This is before the written tradition. It is way back probably hundreds of years and still in the memory of the old storytellers. Do you have any comments on that? Do we know of such a thing? Do you know of any people involved?

Calum a'Chal: I wish I'd brought my great-great-grandfather, 'cause he was one of them. He died in 1881. He was 94 when he died. And his brother Iain Donn in Buaile nam Bodach, he was 95 when he died. They gave quite a few stories to Alexander Carmichael, John Francis Campbell and Hector MacLean. In Iain Donn's case he gave the story of Deirdre which is a bit of a classic. When Carmichael went to visit my great-great-grandfather in Kentangaval and he told him that he had been down to visit his brother in Buaile nam Bodach and that he got a wonderful story. My great-great-grandfather asked what story his brother had given him. He said: "It's the story of Deirdre." And he said: "Well, if you've got the story of Deirdre from my brother, you've never got the story of Deirdre, you've got a fragment." He was very critical about his brother's ability of telling stories. That fragment that they took from Iain Donn was considered a classic folktale. So it makes you wonder whether they had time to take down the full story. He was quite caustic in his comments about his brother, strangely enough. And he says: "I was one day ceilidhing in the house of my brother Iain and he was in the middle of telling a story and I had to walk out with a vexation with the mess he was making of the grand old tale." Something that I found interesting about that comment is that Carmichael asked him if he had the Lay of Deirdre. And he said that he did not have the Lay of Deirdre and he knew only of one person, Donald MacPhee, the smith in Brevig, who was originally from Benbecula, and he was the only man that he knew of the Lay of Deirdre. And he told Carmichael that lays were like stories, they were an Art and only certain people had them. Storytellers weren't these people. The people who told the lays were a separate entity. So everybody had his own trade. He knew that because the smith, Donald MacPhee, was one of his neighbours in Brevig. In that spell my great-great-grandfather was living in Brevig. So he would have known him quite well and he knew that he had a tale.

But the storytelling I do remember in the old village, too. There were storytellers. They were old men when I was a young child, and they were certainly full of stories. Not many of them true. There was a man who died next door to me. I remember when he was on his death bed I used to call in to the woman who stayed in the same house. He was never off his death bed since the day he was born because he was so lazy according to her. He was an old man. Myself and the lad next door we called in before we went to school. He was lying on his bed what we called the closaid in the standard house. He was lying there smoking a pipe. He wouldn't stay on his legs. Somebody said he was just getting old, but the woman said: "No, he has always been like that. He is just too lazy to stay on his legs." And we used to sail wee boats up his knees and down the other side to see if he was awake. He was a wonderful storyteller. He would sit all day and tell stories to kids and anybody.

Q: Where did he get them from?

Calum a'Chal: Well, if you trace his ancestors back, they belong to the Isle of Sandray. But he didn't. And he had a granduncle, Niall Mhìcheil Ruairidh, who had actually gone to Cape Breton. He belonged to Gleann. He was one of these people who never married; probably he didn't want to marry.

He would leave the house to tend lambs at lambing time on a Sunday after mass. He never came back 'til midnight. In that period he went up the hill but he never went very far. Just to the westside of Tangusdale and down to Borve. He'd be there telling his stories, smoking the pipe and drinking tea. And then he'd come back at night. That was his night out. He had been at sea on a fishing patrol vessel and he had been in the Navy. I remember his funeral. They had to take him out of the back window. The rooms were so small, they couldn't take the coffin round. He was quite a tall man. They had to take the bottom off the window to take the coffin out. But there were so many mourners; we used to walk the coffin to church. Coffins used to be walked to church. And then they would be driven from the church to the cemetery. There were a lot of people attending funerals and they would walk to the cemetery. There was a large amount of people that was there waiting at the house, they went along the whole of the Nasg road to the crossroads. So he was well thought of. I never checked what age he was when he died. He was just an old man to me. In the other part of the village there was a man and he was the last man to see the fairy wedding on the island of Hellisay. He was born there in 1855 and he died in 1950 in Nasg. He had lots of stories and tales. It must be of the fairy variety.

Q: Fairy wedding?
Calum a'Chal: Fairy wedding. He swore by it. He said that he'd been to a fairy wedding in the Sìthean, the fairy dell, in Hellisay. The man is featured in the Coddy's book but he is not named. His name was Angus MacKinnon. He was referred to by the East coast fishermen as "Lucky Angus" because he proved to be a lucky hand on the boat.

Q: Any more about fairies?
Calum a'Chal: There was a man who came from Bruernish, a carpenter. He didn't believe in any of this stuff. This man went to visit Angus who was getting old. He didn't believe in the fairies when he went to visit him, but certainly before he left he did. So he managed to convince him. When he died there was a wake. When Angus died an old sparring partner came over as he was being coffined. He had not been told to the last minute. This generally didn't happen. When someone died they would have a wake. Next day they would put the body in a coffin and take it to church. But they didn't tell this man near the village. He got wind of it somehow because he noticed that everybody was walking over to Nasg. So he got wind of it. And he came over after them so see

what was going on. And they were just about to coffin Angus MacKinnon. And when he came through the door and saw his old sparring partner being put in the coffin he shouts to them: "Hold on a minute I'll give the man one last punch." (Sound of a clap) [Laughter]. The reason that he wasn't invited to the wake was because of an incident at a previous wake. The man's wife didn't like milking the cattle. And he had to go through the village of Nasg and milk the cattle. And this was women's work as far as the men were concerned. So he went through the village every day to milk the cow and back again. When he was still alive his cousin's husband used to be laughing and make snide comments and this was getting to him. Of course he couldn't sort him out because it was his cousin's husband. This time the cousin's husband passed away and of course they had a wake. They used to clothe the dead in a long shirt prior to being coffined. Anyway during the wake they were having a few drams. Somewhere along the line he had one or two too many and the younger fellows in the group were winding him up about his cousin's husband because he never got even with him. They were just winding him up. But, of course, you know, he took the bait. And then before the night was out and the remains were lying on the bier, he turned him over, lifted up his shirt and spanked him. After that night he was banned from all wakes.

Q: Did Barrafolk travel to St. Kilda?

Calum a'Chal: There was a woman from St Kilda who died in Barra about in the 1870s. She was working for MacGillivary as a weaveress down in Eoligarry House. She probably came to Barra with the Harris connection that MacGillivary had. In St Kilda there is a place called Geodha Chlann Nèill where a Barra boat is supposed to have been wrecked. It could just have been adrift and happened to get wrecked in that creek. The only other thing is that the fulmar here was always referred to as the Guga Hirteach, the St Kilda gannet. You see a number of fulmars now but they weren't as plentiful even in my own young days as they are now. They were only at the west side of Beinn Tangabhal where you would see them but now they are everywhere. They are in Muldoanich and various other places.

A Note on Calum a'Chal, the *seanachaidh*

by Ian R. Macneil

Calum Macneil, better known as Calum a'Chal, a native Barrach, is a *seanachaidh*. He has long and thoroughly immersed himself in the history – written and oral – of the Barra and Vatersay community in which he is a fisherman and crofter and is much involved in community affairs.

Seanachaidh is used here in the sense of *historian* rather than *reciter of tales* or *recorder* (Dwelly: 1977, 798-99), as in one of the questions asked of Calum a'Chal. I daresay the old bards would have laughed scornfully at these distinctions. Perhaps their origins lie not in the Gaelic but in translation to a modern English influenced by centuries of objectivism. (Neil MacAlpine, whose dictionary ante-dated Dwelly's by seventy-five years, seems to have been less affected by Enlightenment objectivism than was the later Dwelly – an Englishman, not a native Gaelic speaker. MacAlpine includes only *reciter of tales* and *recorder* without reference to *historian* (MacAlpine 1973:220).)

It is curious how human concepts move in circles through time; witness many current post-modernists who insist that there is no history whatever except wholly subjective *story* or *narrative*. Even the ancient bards would never have gone that far – they lived too deeply involved in a hard real world. What is it that seems to make the human mind incapable of living with the tension of two sound yet irreconcilable concepts, and instead constantly insisting on one to the exclusion of the other? The human world is impossibly subjective and impossibly objective. Of course, each human knows, indeed creates, his or her 'objective' world only through and by his or her perceptions. Hence everything is subjective to each of us. Equally of course, for all practical human purposes there is an objective world really out there which any human ignores only at peril of rapid extinction. So let's get on with it, recognising that everything in historiography is both subjective and objective, and the Devil take the hindmost, as he undoubtedly will.

Calum a'Chal's paper is oral history transcribed. The talk transcribed was not only oral history but pure oral history in two respects. First, it was not merely an adjunct to more formal academic historical writing but stood on its own. Second, and perhaps of greater importance is that, except for questions at the end, no interview process has channeled or otherwise distorted his thoughts or words. It is thus one learned man's perception of the history of his community.

At the Northern Studies meeting Calum prefaced his remarks with a quip very much in the great oral traditions of Gaelic culture: He was speaking without notes because he was afraid that using them would atrophy his brain. As none of the talks presented at the meeting was recorded, as soon as Calum's talk was given it ceased to exist except in the memories of those present. This too fits with tradition: 'If they weren't here they shouldn't hear it.'

Nonetheless, Calum was persuaded to present his talk anew to be taped for the present translation into a different medium. It is the nature of oral history that the second talk cannot have been identical to the first. Unless a speaker pretends successfully that he or she is speaking only to himself, there is always a two-way interplay between the speaker and the audience, even when the audience does nothing but sit quietly and listen.

There thus have to have been subtle and perhaps not so subtle differences between the two talks. The first was presented to an audience the major part of which consisted of strangers to Barra most of whom did not have the Gaelic. The second audience was largely people Calum has known all his life, many of whom speak his native tongue, and some of whom had been present for the first talk. Consider, for example, the comments and questions about landlords – always a highly complex and emotional subject in the Highlands and Islands. How could the chemistry of communication between speaker and audiences possibly have been the same when a 21st century landlord was part of the first audience, but not of the second? Moreover, the sizeable second audience – at least the men in it – were paying Calum the highest possible compliment. They had come to hear him rather than to stay home to watch the long anticipated Celtic-Barcelona football game. That kind of accolade would affect even the most phlegmatic *seanachaidh*.

Thus, what is transcribed here is not the exact talk presented to the Northern Studies meeting. Moreover, a talk transcribed is not a talk, but a written report. Anyone familiar with trial or verbatim transcripts of meetings knows how much is lost and changed in translation from the oral to the written medium. Editing may help restore some of the original essence, but only at the risk of new distortions. In this case the editing has been very light. The small headings at the beginning of paragraphs are written substitutes for the pauses, shifts in tone, emphasis, etc. that speakers use in making transitions.

Further reading

This is not a list of sources for Calum MacNeil's talk, but, except for the two dictionaries, a list of publications selected by the editor for readers wishing to explore further particular subjects Calum a'Chal has addressed. Their contents range from folk tales to formal academic work aimed by their authors at as great objectivity as the human condition permits. Which is which and how subjective or objective each is must be left to the subjective judgment of each reader.

Branigan, Keith, 2005, *From Clan to Clearance: History and Archaeology on the Isle of Barra c. 850 - 1850 AD*. Oxford.

Branigan, Keith, & Patrick Foster, 2002, *Barra and the Bishop's Isles: Living on the Margin*. Stroud.

Bumsted, J.M, 1982, *The People's Clearance, 1770-1815*. Edinburgh.

Campbell, John Lorne, ed., Compton MacKenzie, & Carl Hjalmar Borgstrøm, 1936, *The Book of Barra*. London

Campbell, Dr. J.L. & Constance Eastwick, 1966, 'The Macneils of Barra in the Forty-five,' *Innes Review,* 17:82

Chambers, Anne, 1998, *Granuaile, The Life and Times of Grace O' Malley, c. 1530-1603*, rev ed. Dublin.

Dwelly, Edward, 1977, *The Illustrated Gaelic-English Dictionary, 1901-11*. Glasgow.

Hunter, James, 1976, *The Making of the Crofting Community*.

MacAlpine, Neil, 1973, *Pronouncing Gaelic-English Dictionary*, 1832. Glasgow.

Macneil of Barra, Robert Lister, 1923, *The Clan Macneil*. New York.

MacPherson, John, 1960, *Tales from Barra Told by the Coddy*. Edinburgh.

Newby, Andrew, 1998-2000, 'Emigration and Clearance from the Island of Barra, c. 1770-1858,' *Transactions Gaelic Society of Inverness*, 61:116

Richards, Eric, 2000, *The Highland Clearances: People Landlords & Rural Turmoil*.

Walker, John, 1980, Margaret M McKay, ed, *The Rev. Dr. John Walker's Report on the Hebrides of 1764 & 1771*. Edinburgh.

On the Verge of Loss: Lesser Known Place-names of Barra and Vatersay

Anke-Beate Stahl

BARRA can be reached by various means of transport. The traditional way is by boat. The first settlers must have arrived by boat; the Norse came by boat, the Admiralty as they chased Bonnie Prince Charlie across the Hebrides travelled of course by boat, as do the majority of tourists today. The view from the ferry as it carefully navigates the curve into Castlebay is usually the first impression one has of Barra: a picturesque rocky bay surrounded by villages and hills scattered with houses. No doubt the most spectacular way to travel to Barra is by plane and on a clear day it reveals a stunning view onto the maze of hidden bays, rocks and deserted islands. Many of them have names but nowadays not many people know them.

Maps and charts of Barra give evidence of 500 officially recorded place-names covering the most prominent natural features and settlements. Between 1995 and 1999 a total of 97 inhabitants of Barra and Vatersay contributed more than 2000 previously unmapped place-names, thus helping recreate parts of the place-name fabric that once covered the entire group of islands. A number of gaps on the map could be closed and names of less prominent sites and features could be traced down to the some of the smallest microtoponymics. During the collection, discussions arose regarding the quality of names – for example, should a place-name that was used or remembered by only one family qualify to as a name in its own right? The question arose as to whether a name had to be used for a certain length of time before it was worthy of being entered into the collection. This in turn could have questioned the validity of including features that had been named but that had since physically disappeared as a result of erosion or disuse. Would their names be less valuable than younger names? The quality or credibility of a name was most often questioned when it was only one of several names for a particular feature, alternative names having been given by various ethnic groups or, as in the case of younger names on Barra, by inhabitants of different townships.

The following definition of the term *name* formed the terminological base for the collection and examination of Barra's place-names:

> A place-name is a label that in its spoken and written form designates an identified location, real or imaginary, and reflects the culture and history of an area. The application of a label to a user's association of place eases reference and provides a basis for communication.

This paper presents a selection of place-names which for various reasons may have changed their names, become obsolete or have never been entered on a map in the first place. This includes features for which there are several alternative names, prominent features whose names have been forgotten and places whose naming was inspired by an incident or a story. The names are discussed clockwise round the island and are grouped according to their geographic location.

The West

One of the most prominent lochs on the west side, *Loch Tangasdail* (NL645998), has five competing names. The specific *Tangasdal* is derived from ON *tangi*, m, 'headland' and possibly from Old Norse (ON) *dalr*, m, 'valley' and is the name of the township on whose land the loch is located. The 1991 Ordnance Survey (OS) Pathfinder Map, however, lists two names for this location: *Loch Tangusdale* in its pre-Gaelicized spelling and *Loch St Clair*. The name *Loch St Clair* was an invention of a Victorian novelist which found its way onto the maps[1] but is no longer mentioned on the 2003 OS Explorer map although it still appears to be used among some locals. Another name for the same feature is *Loch MhicLèoid*, 'MacLeod's loch', a name very likely to have been inspired by the remains of the tower located on the picturesque island in the loch, *Dùn Mhic Leòid* (NL647996). The late Roderick MacNeil, whose croft in Kinloch adjoined the loch, remembered that the "tower was built by a Maclean, Iain Garbh, and he was the son of Mor nan Ceann. He came to Barra with her. [...] They lived at first in Castle Kisimul and then he built that castle

---

1   I am grateful to Roderick MacNeil (Ruairidh Fhionnlaigh) for this piece of information.

for himself there. The island is artificial." However, no explanation was given as to why the tower was named after MacLeod and not after MacLean, who built it. Some people call this loch *An Loch Mòr* 'the large lake' which suggests that there must be a comparatively smaller loch nearby. And indeed, just 300m northwest lies *Loch na Doirlinn* 'lake of the isthmus', whose alternative name is *An Loch Beag* 'the small lake'. The fifth and least known name is *Loch an Eas Dhuibhe* 'lake of the dark waterfall'.[2] The location of this lake at the bottom of the steep slope of *Beinn Tangabhal*, with two streams running from the hillside into the lake, contributes to the credibility of this name although no informant was able to identify the location of the 'dark waterfall' on the map.

Travelling north just past the Isle of Barra Hotel and before the turn-off to Borgh lies a small stony bay on the left hand side of the road. There are two little rocky points jutting into the sea but only one of them made its way onto the map. Its name, *Stoung Mòr* (NF650013), is paralleled by its smaller counterpart, *Stoung Beag* (NF652011) a name remembered by just one informant. It is derived from ON *stöng*, f, 'mast' which is a popular place-name element in Norway for islands and peninsulas. Whereas *Tràigh Tuath* 'north beach' at the outskirts of Baile na Creige and the mouth of may be a name remembered for its association with dangerous quicksand, one of the most dramatic and picturesque beaches of the island, at the foot of Beinn Mhartainn just below Father MacMillan's cottage, could no longer be remembered by name. Its mapped name, *Tràigh Hamara* is a Gaelic Norse hybrid and has the meaning of 'beach of the steep rock' from the ON generic *hamarr*, m, 'steep rock' or 'steep hillside'. Its exposed location at the Atlantic coast led to much of the adjoining land being washed away in the January gales of 2005. Erosion, consequent loss of land and an inevitably changing coastline is a sad reality for Barra's westside.

The North-west

The old coffin carriers' route, *Ciste na Clìthe* 'pass of the cliff' used to run from Cliaid to Suidheachan and ended at the graveyard of Cille Bharra in Barra's north saving the carriers a four-mile detour on the conventional road. During the strenuous walk the coffin carriers took regular breaks, and the resting places along the path received names. Contrary to popular belief the first element of this name, *ciste* is not related to Gaelic *cist*, f, a loanword from Latin cista,

---

2   The name was initially collected by the father of the present chief MacNeil of MacNeil from a local Barraman.

'chest, coffin'. The name in its current grammatical constellation strongly suggests a derivation from the ON place-name generic *kista*, f, 'pass', 'narrowing'.[3]

One of the names along this path is *Coireachan 'ic Nèill* 'MacNeil's kettle stand' (NF681052). The large stones at this site form a circle and are said to have been the hearth for a gigantic kettle owned by the MacNeil of Barra whose supposedly grand lifestyle was occasionally ridiculed by the local population. *Dùnan Ruadh* 'red little fort' (NF683054) is an alternative name of *Dùn Chliobh* 'fort of the cliff' which is a mapped name. *Leac nan Leannan* 'flagstone of the lovers' (NF674048) is a reminder of the tragic story of two underaged lovers who escaped their followers on horseback. Approaching the rocks at the cliff, the horse slipped and the lovers and the horse fell and died. *Spòg a' Deamhainn* 'the devil's paw' depicts a rock on which the devil supposedly left his footprint. It is in immediate vicinity of *The Lamb's Footprints* (NF680051) which is listed in the Maclean manuscript 8233 as *Leac Luirg* 'flagstone of the footprint'[4]. *Creag Labhar* at the northwest end of Tràigh Chliaid (NL626963) has the meaning of 'speaking rock'. Sound is an element that is rarely used in naming. In this case sound may have been created by water running over the rock or by noise caused by strong wind. Legend has it that "one day when a procession passed, the man in the coffin spoke and said that the rock would fall one day on a MacNeil woman. Hence its name."[5]

Nowadays coffins are transported in hearses and the original motivation to use the path no longer exists. Only the occasional hill-walker walks along this route, the track has faded and is in most parts no longer traceable. Here, too, the coastline is subject to heavy erosion and some of the named features along the path can no longer be identified, whilst others may have disappeared into the sea.

Another rock, only three kilometres east of Leac Labhar, is *Clach Mhòr nan Gleannan* 'big rock of the little valleys' (NF702047). In the Ordnance Survey Object Name Book, the original hand written collection of place-names to be suggested for entry on maps, the stone is described as a "large ice-carried

---

3   See Cox, 1987, II:63 and see Rygh, *Norske Gaardnavne*, V:335.

4   Maclean manuscripts, 8233, University of Edinburgh Library, Special Collection.

5   Story by Flora Boyd, Sound Archive of the School of Scottish Studies, Department of Celtic and Scottish Studies, University of Edinburgh, SA 1974/112/A9.

Ciste na Clìthe

boulder on the eastern shoulder of Beinn Eireabhal. It is about 30 feet long, 20 wide and 18 feet high". According to folk-etymology once the stone rolls downhill, Barra will be doomed.[6]

Halfway between Beinn Eireabhal and the caves at Tràigh Chliaid is a small loch just northwest of *Loch Cuilce* 'loch of reeds'. On the map it is nameless but among locals it is known as *Loch an Eich Uisge* 'lake of the kelpie' (NF682046). The story goes that a girl who was herding sheep met a beautiful horse at this loch. She became very friendly with the horse, stroked it and when she eventually mounted it, the horse ran into the loch and the girl was never seen again. Stories of kelpies, water-horses, are told throughout the Highlands and Islands and the common name for these lakes -as in Barra- is *Loch an Eich Uisge*. In Scottish folktales kelpie lakes and haunted shielings are often situated close to each other and this is also the case in Barra. *Àirigh na h-Aon Oidhche* 'shieling of the one night' (NF703037) is located less than 500m

---

6   Ordnance Survey Object Name Book, Barra Parish, 1878, Scottish Record Office, Edinburgh, RH4/23/106.

Clach Mhòr nan Gleannan

to the north east of Loch an Eich Uisge and is a place where visitors hardly dared to stay longer than one night.[7]

The caves at Tràigh Chliaid, *Uamh Chliaid* (NF673049), are said to be another haunted site. There are several stories of underground passages leading from the caves in Cliaid to other caves on the island even as far as *Uamh an Oir* 'gold cave' (NL682972) at Rubha Mòr, a large headland in the south-east of Barra. Various people are said to have been lost in the passages, including a piper whose bagpipes, according to legend, can still be heard around Loch an Dùin. His accompanying dog, however, managed to return – hairless.

The North

The northern part of Barra is less haunted[8] and its naming is straightforward. *Vaslain* (NF693054), an area which inspired the secondary name *Beinn*

---

7   According to Ronald Black in folklore this place-name is generally connected with a kelpie who attacked the inhabitants of the shieling in order to suck their blood, just like vampires.

\8   With exception of Eòlaigearraidh Primary School which is reported to have a presence.

Bhaslain, was mentioned in the Craigston Register of Births, Marriages and Deaths[9] as early as 1823. Its name is derived from the genitive case of ON *vatn*, n, 'water' and ON *land*, n, 'piece of land'. *Suidheachan* 'seats' (NF688055) is the name of the former shell factory at the Tràigh Mhòr and was initially built by Compton MacKenzie, the author of Whisky Galore. As is often the case with house names, inspiration was taken from a nearby natural feature. *Suiachan*, just a few hundred metres west of the building, used to be one of the coffin carriers' traditional resting places.

A feature which most visitors of Tràigh Eais, the large beach opposite the airfield, come across is called *Stobs a' Bhodaich* 'fence posts of the old man' (NF695067) which are at the very end of the main path leading towards the Atlantic. The 'old man' in question is Michael MacLean, a former grazing constable, who erected wooden fences as protection from erosion.[10] One of the very few names including a preposition is found not far from this spot. *Eadar an Dà Bheinn* 'between the two mountains' (NF704071), is also known as *Bealach an Dà Bheinn* 'pass of the two mountains' and is likely to have been the old main footpath leading from Sgùrabhal and Eòlaigearraidh to the local primary school. This path is located between *Beinn Eòlaigearraidh* 'mountain of E.' (NF701072) and *Beinn Bheag Eòlaigearraidh* 'small mountain of E.'(NF705071), or as locals call it *A' Bheinn Mhòr* 'the large mountain' and 'the small mountain', *A' Bheinn Bheag*. The more familiar people are with their surroundings the fewer specifics are required in naming of their local natural features. This is also the case with a stretch of shore which inhabitants of Sgùrabhal and Eòlaigearraidh call Mol Sgùrabhail or simplified A' *Mhol*, a loan from ON *möl*, f, 'gravel bed' (NF695084).

Nowadays its official map name is Gaelic (G) *Bàgh nan Clach* 'bay of stones', a descriptive term for the beach which is entirely covered in stones and pebbles of varying sizes. The earliest written record of this area can be traced back to 1874 when the Admiralty charted this area - unsurprisingly in English language – as *Stoney Bay*.[11] This name is the only name in the entire Barra

---

9   Roman Catholic Diocese of Argyll and the Isles Records, 1805/1944, Craigston, Scottish Record Office, Edinburgh, RH21/50/1, 2, 3.

10   I am grateful to Michael MacKinnon (Michel Nialtaidh) for supplying this information.

11   See 1861-62 Admiralty Chart no. 2770 "Scotland West Coast, Hebrides, Sound of Barra", small corrections in 1874, scale 1:15000.

Beinn Sgùrabhail

group[12] which means exactly the same in all three languages involved in the naming process, English, Gaelic and Old Norse.

Sgùrabhal the name of the northernmost settlement of Barra (NF700092) is likely to have undergone significant contraction. Borgstrøm who carried out a linguistic analysis of the Gaelic dialect of Barra derives this name from the ON Skaga-rif-fjall 'hill near the reef of the promontory'[13]. While a descriptive name for this important shipping mark appears logical, it is not possible at this stage to definitively identify the meaning of the first element of this name. Possible interpretations include a derivation from ON *skör*, f, 'prominent hill', or a link to ON *skor*, f, 'cleft', which if used in its plural form *skora* would translate as 'hill of the clefts', which, too, would make onomastic sense in this location.

Names such as *Gob Sgùrabhail, Beinn Sgùrabhail, Tràigh Sgùrabhail and Dun Sgùrabhail* form part of a name cluster, a naming strategy which is rarely used in Barra but which is common on the mainland. Name clusters

---

12 I define the Barra group as all islands between the Sound of Barra and Barra Head.

13 Borgstrøm, 1937:292.

indicate that an area received its names within a relatively short period of time. Indeed the north of Barra, one of the most fertile areas on the island, was at one stage cleared to make way for a large farm with *Eoligarry House,* also known as *An Taigh Geal 'the white house'* or *An Taigh Mòr 'the big house'* (NF703077) at its centre. In the Parish Register of Barra, reference is made to four settlements that were formerly located in that area. They are *Vaslain, Chiall, Kilbar* and *Eòlaigearraidh.* The name that appears least frequently in the register,

Eòlaigearraidh,[14] nowadays refers to the whole district of North Barra, whereas the names of other settlements in that area are in danger of falling into disuse. Although the area in which *Chiall* is located is inhabited and its name is mentioned on the OS map (NF717067), it is no longer used as a landmark for local orientation. The name *Vaslain* is a combination of ON *vatn,* n, 'water' and ON *land,* n, 'piece of land' (NF694055) and means 'wet land'. The name occurs in earlier forms as *Vaslan (1823)* and *Vaslin (1825).* The place was still inhabited by a shepherd in 1878, but is nowadays an empty stretch of land. *Scalavaslain* (NF687057) is the name of a nearby hill which contains the settlement name Vaslain, but with the decline of intensive land use, the names of smaller elevations are increasingly falling into disuse and Scalavaslain, too, can be expected to be forgotten once it disappears from the map. *Kilbar,* once the name of the local church and of the entire district of North Barra, has now been reduced to only the name of the church and a street called *Cille Bharra,* but in contrast to Vaslain and Chiall, it is still part of the postal address. The dominance of the name *Eòlaigearraidh* was made possible in 1919, when *Eòlaigearraidh Farm* was raided and eventually purchased by the Ministry of Agriculture and Fisheries. The land was divided into crofts and the postal address has since consisted of the croft number and the name *Eòlaigearraidh.* Although residents of Barra are fully aware where *Sgùrabhal* is, its written representation is neither reflected in the postal address nor the local telephone directory, nor in any place-name signs in the village.

The North-east

The journey leads back via the rocky, indented East coast.

Due to the new ferry link between Barra and Eriskay the peninsula of *Aird Mhòr* meaning 'large headland' (NF713039), formerly a cul-de-sac, has recently become a major traffic hub on the island. Places, once almost forgotten, are now

---

14   Or in variations of its Anglicized spelling 'Eoligarry'.

passed by many people on a daily basis. One of the former inhabitants of this peninsula, Ronald MacKinnon, known as Raogan, was particularly knowledgeable on place-names of this area. Due to his contribution the point immediately north of the new jetty can be identified as *Rubha Carraig nan Coineanach*, 'promontory of the fishing-rock of the rabbits' (NF720040) the area south of it as *Rubha Pheadair*, 'Peter's point' (NF723037) and the site of the jetty itself as *Carraig nan Coineanach*, 'fishing-rock of the rabbits' (NF721039).[15]

Aird Mhidhnis, the headland south of Aird Mhòr is immediately associated with the fish factory. Jonathan MacNeil (Eoin Feannag), a local of this peninsula, pointed out a place he remembers being called *Cnoc na Brataich* 'hill of the flag' (NF716033). Here a flag used to be raised to announce the arrival of herring shoals. Those among the temporary curers who lived on the west side of Barra only had to walk as far as *Beul an Fheadain* (NF683033) just west of Loch an Dùin, from which the flag was visible, to find out whether their work was required. If it is was, the flag would be raised. This simple measure prevented west coast people from walking all the way to Aird Mhidhnis in vain.

Drochaid nan Coineanach 'bridge of the rabbits' (NF710038) is located on the right hand side just before the Aird Mhidhnis road swings back round to merge with the main road and *Tobar nan Coineanach* 'well of the rabbits' (NF709037) is located on the left hand side of the road. Leaving the Aird Mhidhnis road and waiting to turn onto the main road one's eye is immediately drawn to a green patch of land midway up Beinn Eireabhail, the grey rocky hill straight ahead. This place is known as *Na Horgh* 'heap of stones', 'cairn' (NF704040) from ON *hörgr* and in Norway this element usually depicts important sites of heathen worship.[16] Nowadays it is difficult to imagine that this almost forgotten spot, and the densely inhabited council house estate of *Horogh* (NL657970) whose name undoubtedly derives from the same stem, must have been sites of extraordinary religious importance.

The very small and yet striking island (NF706032) in the harbour of *Bàgh a Tuath, Northbay*, was given a total of five different names. The island which is too small to be of any economic use, and too far inland to serve as a nautical point, is visible form the main road junction connecting the East and West roads

---

15 Ronald MacKinnon passed away in December 1995 just days before his third interview. He
    placed more than 150 formerly unrecorded names on the map.

16 See Rygh, 1898:57.

with the northern route to the airport. This island is known as *Eilean nan Gèadh* 'geese island', *Eilean nan Rodan* 'island of the rats', possibly after sightings of the animals in question, *Eilean na Craoibh* 'tree island', after its vegetation and in contrast to the remaining bare rocks in the harbour, *An t-Eilean Beag* 'small island', a descriptive and obvious choice and the undoubtedly youngest name among the five, *Statue Island,* as it is home to a statue of St. Barr created by Northbay artist Margaret Somerville in 1975.

    Bruairnis is the largest of the three headlands in the north-east. Its name is a combination of ON *brúar*, f, gen, 'bridge' and ON *nes*, n, 'headland' and is clearly named after man-made construction to help people pass the muddy dip between Bruairnis and Bogach. The headland itself has three striking elevations on which there are cairns with *Beinn nan Càrnan* 'mountain of the cairns'(NF727011) to the south, *An Cnoc Mòr* 'the big hill' (NF730013) in middle position and *Meall na Meadhanach* (NF727017) to the north. G meadhanach is usually translated as 'middle'. Although Meall na Meadhanach is clearly not in middle of the three hills, its specific may refer to its position relative to other nearby hills. The cairns on the three hills will have played some part in orienteering but it is not clear whether they were used as fishing marks or in order to help pilots find their way to the Tràigh Mhòr airfield. As with many villages on Barra and Vatersay the main settlement on this peninsula is named after the natural feature in whose proximity it is located. *Rubha Chàrnain*, the 'stony promontory' (NF723025), designates the rocky stretch of shore used by boats as a navigation guide as they enter Bàgh Shiarabhagh and used also to be the name for what is now known as Lower Bruernish. The upper part of Bruairnis is known among locals as *Cnoc nan Caorach*, 'sheep hill' (NF725019). The entire area received its nickname 'Little England' because it was a favourite among English holiday homebuyers in the 1960s who may have encouraged the use of English names for the upper and the lower part of the village. Like Eolaigearraidh and Vatersay Bruairnis suffered from a complete loss of population during the clearances.

The East

The name *Buaile nam Bodach* 'milking-place of the old men' (NF713015) was first recorded in 1814 as *Bualenanbodach* and appeared on the Admiralty Chart in 1874 as *Old Mans Fold*. Legend has it that

MacNeil of Barra's wife was through the buaile (fold) when the women were milking. It was the custom to offer a drink to anyone who passed but for some reason she was not offered it. She cried at the top of her voice: "Bithidh fein Buaile nam Bodach!", 'May yourselves be the fold of the old men!', which was understood to predict for them belated marriages, and unhappy homes afterwards.[17]

Loch nic Ruaidhe (NF702018), also known as *Loch na h-Ighne Ruaidhe*, 'loch of the red-haired girl' and *Loch na h-Ighne Bàine*, 'loch of the fair-haired girl' is a rather large loch located in the hills above Loch na h-Obe Cottage. The specific of the name refers to a red-haired girl who supposedly lived at this place and who fell in love with the son of the MacNeil of Barra. When the girl became pregnant, she and her lover escaped by boat and are said to have settled on Colonsay.

Lochan nam Faoileann (NF709014) refers collectively to two lochs located just above the radio transmitter in Buaile nam Bodach. The G word *faoileann* means 'common seagull', 'mew'. However, a derivation from ON *vaðill*, m, 'ford', seems onomastically more appropriate and the G name may have developed as a result of folk-etymology. Dwelly lists *fadhail*, f, with the meaning of 'ford' which suits the geographical setting perfectly as there is a little ford between the two lochs. Locals distinguish between *Loch na Fadhlainn Àrd* and *Loch na Fadhlainn Ìseal*, the 'high' and the 'low loch of the ford'.

Past the township of Buaile nam Bodach at Rubha Lìos lies another loch and at least one of its competing names is of historical interest. Some people call this lake *Loch an Rubha*, 'loch of the promontory', (NF706007) due to its proximity to Rubha Lìos. Others name it after its vegetation *Loch nan Lilies* 'loch of the water lilies' or a name with a less distinctive specific, *Loch nan Flùraichean*, 'loch of the flowers'. The official Ordnance Survey (OS) name - but probably least known - is *Loch Scotageary*. The specific element of this name refers to the settlement *Scotagearraidh* (NF711004) which is said to have been cleared within 24 hours. Whereas foundations of houses can still be traced, nowadays only one family remembered that a settlement by this name ever existed. The generic of this name is derived from ON *gerði*, n, 'enclosure', 'fenced field', 'garden'. The meaning of its specific, however, is uncertain. It may be associated with G *sgot*, m, 'small farm' or 'small flock', which combined with the above generic would result in 'enclosure of the small flock'

---

17   Farquhar MacRae, Maclean manuscripts, P.8103.

or 'enclosure of the small farm'. Nevertheless the word order with the generic in second position points rather at a specific of Old Norse origin. Heggstad[18] lists the ON noun *skot*, n, 'projectile', 'shot'. Eysteinnson derives the similar looking specific of the Harris place-name Scotasay from ON *skot*, 'neuk', 'corner'[19], which would also match the geographic location of this name.

The South-east

Allt Heisgeir (NF695006) is a confluence of two rivulets in the valley between Bheinn Ghunaraigh and Thartabhal, and its mouth marks the northern boundary of Earsairidh. Old forms of this name are *Aulthaichair* (1823) and *Allt Haichair* (1901). Whereas the first element, *'allt'*, is Gaelic and means 'stream', its second element may be of ON but is obscure. The commonly used form of this name is its shortened form *Allt*.

 Halfway House is a low-lying cottage in Earsairidh and its location marks the exact midpoint of the journey between Bruairnis and Castlebay. This name was coined in the days when walking long distances was the rule and parts of the journey had to be broken down into measurable units.

 One place may have several competing names which were inspired either by different ethnic groups inhabiting the same area, or given by members sharing the same cultural background but living in different communities. In Barra it is not unusual to find several different names in use for one geographical feature. In all known cases these entities are located on or close to township boundaries and consequently must have been in the geographical scope of at least two communities. A local from Gearraidh Gadhal remembered three different names for a bay located south-west of Beinn nan Càrnan: *Bàgh na Teileagraf*, 'telegraph bay' (NL690973), *Port a' Bhuailte*, 'bay of the hut', and *Bàgh Hòraid*, a name with an obsolete specific. The first name, *Bàgh na Teileagraf* can be directly linked to Barra's telegraph connection, which was established in 1884, and is probably the youngest name of the three. *Port a' Bhuailte* is the name that residents of the township of Gearraidh Gadhal applied to the place, whereas people living on the north side of Beinn nan Càrnan in Brèibhig used *Bàgh Hòraid*, a name most likely of ON origin.

---

18 L. Heggstad, 1930:610.

19 O. Eysteinnson, 1992.

Halfway House

The South

A name may fall out of use although the place continues to exist. In other cases a name can survive, although the feature it originally referred to may be less and less used and eventually disappear. In Barra this is the case with a stretch of the old road leading from Breibhig to Castlebay. Whereas the new road branches off left to lead down to the village of Castlebay, the old and now overgrown, but still visible, footpath leads to Castlebay via Gleann. Although very few people walk the old path, its name, *An Leathad Cas* 'the steep slope'(NL676988), is still known by locals.

The south is dominated by Barra's capital, Castlebay, which stretches around a sheltered bay at the foot of the island's largest hill, Sheabhal. Here the name of the village has been taken from the major natural feature nearby. The

Castlebay

village of *Castlebay* has two alternative names, *Baile MhicNèill* 'MacNeil's village', a name listed in Dwelly and remembered by some very old local informants, and *Bàgh a' Chaisteil*, the Gaelic translation of 'Castlebay'. The earliest documentation for the name *Castle Bay*, the name actually depicting the bay and not the village, dates back to 1854. An earlier entry on the Maclean map of 1823 calls this area *Kissimul Bay*. *Kisimul*, the rock on which the castle stands, was mentioned for the first time in 1549 as *Kiselnin* and in 1695 as *Kisimul*. The essential clue to solving the derivation of the first part of this name was supplied by Father Allan McDonald, priest of Eriskay, in a list of names dating back to 1903.[20] Here he gives *Ciasmul* as an alternative spelling which points at a derivation from ON *kjóss*, m, 'small bay' and ON *múli*, m, 'headland' or more appropriate in this case 'sea-rock'. Kisimul, 'rock of the small bay', provides an accurate geographic setting for this derivation. Another term for the same rock is *A' Steinn*, a name remembered by the late Malcolm MacAulay, who belonged to an old family of tradition bearers in Castlebay[21]. *A' Steinn* derives from ON *steinn*, m, and may be translated as 'stones that cannot be moved', 'hill', 'rock', and, as in this location, 'small rocky island'.

---

20   A. McDonald 1901-03:432f.

21   Malcolm MacAulay, Sound Archive, Celtic and Scottish Studies, School of Literatures, Languages and Cultures, University of Edinburgh, SA1976/9.

There are a number of rocks at the entrance to Castle Bay and in the bay itself that deserve further discussion. An important nautical marker for boats entering and leaving Castle Bay is the beacon rock which appears on maps as *Sgeir Dubh*, G for 'dark skerry'. Local fishermen, however, call this rock *Dubhsgeir*, an inversion of Sgeir Dubh (NL667967). Travelling around the bay in an anticlockwise direction there is the small island of *Orasaigh*, on which another *An Taigh Geal* (NL666971), 'the white house' was located. The southerly tip of Orasaigh is called *An Rubha Dubh*, 'the dark point'. There are four islands in the Barra group alone called Orasaigh. They all share the same geographical peculiarity, i.e. being an island at high tide and being connected to a larger island at low tide. This is reflected in the name which is translated as 'ebbtide island', a combination of ON *órför*, f, 'ebbtide' and ON *ey*, f, 'island'. *Orasaigh*, or in its Anglicised spelling *Orosay* or *Oronsay* are frequently occurring place-names in the Western Isles, Norway and in Iceland. The small rock to the west of Orasaigh is *Innisgeir* (NL664972) whose generic is clearly derived from ON *sker*, n, 'skerry'. Its first element is likely to be of ON origin but cannot be clearly identified. There is *Eilean nan Rodan* 'island of rats', just south of *Leigemul* (NL665975) whose first element is obscure. Its generic - as in Kisimul - is based on ON *múli*, m, 'headland', or here 'rock surrounded by the sea'. The small rocks between the castle and Leadaig are called *Sgeirean Cùil a' Bhaile*, 'skerries at the neuk of the village', or simply *Na Sgeirean* (NL666978). *Bun na h-Aibhne*, 'mouth of the river' (NL669981), depicts the area at which *An t-Allt Ruadh* 'the red stream' (NL673982) runs into the bay. This river has various names depending on its location in the village. Its upper section is *Allt a' Ghlinne* 'stream of the valley', which changes into *Allt Alasdair* 'Alexander's stream' and eventually becomes *An t-Allt Ruadh* beside Morag MacNeill's croft.

The stretch of harbour outside the main shopping area of Castlebay is named *Port na h-Àirde* 'port of the promontory' (NL666982) after *An Àird Ghlas* 'the grey headland' (NL666983) at the foot of which the ferry terminal, the post office and the bank are located. This area used to be *called Cnoc na Féille*, 'market hill', but the market has long gone. Unsurprisingly the names for this area have almost been forgotten. The headland has been so dramatically transformed and built over with houses, shops and tarmac that its original specific, the colour of the headland, is no longer the main distinguishing factor. People orientate themselves by the position of the shops in the street rather than any natural features.

The South-west

The south-west is dominated by one large and several small mountains and a treacherous coastline indented with extremely dangerous *slocs,* the long, narrow, deep inlets carved into the stone by the sea. The highest elevation is *Beinn Tangabhail,* a Gaelic-Norse composition derived from G *beinn,* f, 'mountain' and the ON specific composed of ON *tangi,* m, 'headland' and ON *fjall,* n, mountain. What is now the ON specific would originally have been the full name assigned to the feature with ON *fjall* 'mountain' acting as generic. As over the centuries the ON name became obsolete, and Norse was no longer understood, the name transformed into an onomastic unit and knowledge of its meaning was no longer essential. The original ON name became a specific and the new generic, G *beinn,* 'mountain', was added. *Beinn Tangabhail* also has a purely G alternative name, *A' Bheinn Mhòr* 'the large hill'. A secondary peak, just 200-300m west of the highest one is named *Beinn na Cailliche* 'hill of the old woman' or *A' Bheinn Bhreac* 'speckled hill'. The hill around which the road leading from Nasg to the causeway bends is named after a small loch south-west of its peak. The name of the mountain is *Beinn an Lochain* 'mountain of the small loch' (NL643985) and the name of the loch on the mountain slope is *Loch Bheinn an Lochain* 'loch of *Beinn an Lochain*' or - if the specific is broken up into its components - 'loch of the mountain of the small loch'. In the name of the loch the specific, *Beinn an Lochain,* has become an onomastic unit, a tag, whose meaning is no longer of importance to the name user and therefore the element 'loch' occurs in the name of the loch twice, once as a generic and once as part of the specific, both referring to the same feature.

Looking across to Beinn Tangabhal from Caolas in Vatersay there are patches of particularly green grass sloping down to a sandy beach. These are the remains of a settlement named *Goirtein* from G *goirtean* 'enclosure' (NL635982), a cleared area. Before Barraigh and Bhatarsaigh were connected via a causeway in 1991 cattle used to be swum across Caolas Bhatarsaigh, the 'sound of Vatersay', and regularly landed at *Làimhrig nam Mart* 'landing-place of the cows' (NL634978).

Vatersay (Bhatarsaigh)

Vatersay, the island that lies just south of Barra has had a vivid past and has been home to a number of tragedies, clearances, raid and eventually re-settlement. Its permanent connection to Barra had pros and cons: Before the causeway was built its irregular ferry service to Barra meant that people could not always rely on goods being shipped across on time and they had to make their own way to attend dances and celebrations in Castlebay which in a few occasions resulted in tragic drowning accidents. However, in general the islanders enjoyed a status in which the law was not always as readily enforced as on the its neighbouring island.

The three settlements on Vatersay have straightforward names. *Caolas*, the village to the north of the island, is the Gaelic word for 'sound' (NL633973) and takes its name from the *Sound of Vatersay, Caolas Bhatarsaigh. Uidh*, the most easterly village, is derived from G *uidh*, f, a loan from ON *eið*, f, and means 'isthmus, neck of land' and is a perfect description of its geographic setting. Historic forms of the name include 1823 *Uiehead*, 1833 *Uigh*, 1836 *Aoidh* and 1851 *Uie*. *Bhatarsaigh*, or *Vatersay Village* (NL633943) is the largest settlement and lies in the southern part of the island. An old name for this village is *An Scarp*. There is an island in Harris called An Scarp and the element is also reflected in historic spellings of a neighbouring island in Barra that is now known as *Maol Dòmhnaich*. Earliest written records refer to *Maol Dòmhnaich* as 1549 *Scarpanamutt* and 1654 *Scarpa*. However, the meaning of this element remains obscure.

A chain of mountains dominates the northern part of the island. The highest mountain at 190m is *A' Bheinn Mhòr* 'the big mountain' (NL626964) which appears on Sharbau's estate plan of 1901 as *Bein a' Carnan*, a composition of G beinn, 'mountain' and G càrn, 'cairn, rock, pile of stones'. Its smaller counterpart, *A' Bheinn Bheag* 'little mountain', is 149m high and lies just west of A' Bheinn Mhòr at NL619965. On maps the OS incorrectly list the highest mountain of Vatersay as *Theiseabhal Mòr. Theiseabhal Mòr* is 172m high and lies in fact further east (NL638961) where the OS placed *Theiseabhal Beag* on the maps. This in return lies still further east (NL641962) and is the elevation round which the road to Vatersay Village leads. Whereas the specifics of the previous two mountain names, *beag* and *mòr*, are G and mean 'small' and 'large' respectively, the first element is clearly related to ON *Heistafjall* with ON *hestr*, m, 'horse', and ON *fjall*, n, 'mountain'. It was at the slope of this mountain that a Catalina sea plane crashed on 12th May 1944 with six of the nine crew members surviving the impact. The remains of the plane can still be seen scattered between the road and the shore (NL640956).

Between the peaks of the chain of mountains there are a number of passes which people used as shortcuts. They are particularly visible when travelling from Caolas in a southerly direction. As might be expected the most easterly pass between *Theiseabhal Mòr* and *Theiseabhal Beag* is called *Bealach Theiseabhail* 'pass of Theiseabhail' (NL639963). The pass between Theiseabhal Mòr and A' Bheinn Mhòr has a descriptive name, *Am Bealach Uaine*, 'the green pass' (NL634961). The most prominent pass of this mountain range is *Bealach nan Daoine* 'pass of the people' (NL624964) and separates *Theiseabhal Mòr* to the east and *A' Bheinn Bheag* to the west.

Although Bhatarsaigh has a number of small rivulets there is no substantial lake on the island. The three lochs indicated on the OS map are shallow. Two of them, *Loch Dhòmhnaill a' Bhealaich* 'lake of 'Donald of the Pass" (NL634974) and *Loch Bean Iain* 'lake of Bean Iain (Ian's wife)' (NL632973) lie just beside the road in Caolas, the third one, *Loch Pheigi* 'Peggy's loch' (NL631943) lies at the end of the road in Vatersay Village. Dòmhnaill a' Bhealaich is the nickname of Donald MacDonald who was one of the first people to resettle on the island after its compulsory purchase by the Congested Districts Board from Lady Gordon Cathcart. It is striking that the names of all the lochs on Vatersay have specifics that refer to people, rather than the more common situation where specifics refer to the shape of a loch, vegetation or other natural feature. It would be very interesting to trace the names of the two pools (NL623938 and NL623945) at the slope of Beinn Ruilibreac just south west of Vatersay Village which remain unidentified.

Conclusion

The place-names of Barra and Vatersay give evidence of the inhabitants' history, their perception of their surroundings, their work and social life, their superstitions, customs, beliefs and most of all their attachment to the land. Changes in land use, in climate, social life, technology and transport have all contributed to places being visited less often and their place-names as an inevitable result being on the verge of being forgotten or place-names already lost. But not all is bleak. Work life on Barra has changed dramatically and the arrival of the internet means that more people can choose to stay and work on the island and although most new jobs are being carried out indoors these people will spend at least part of their leisure time outdoors. The internet also facilitates research into and publication of relevant place-name material which can be accessed by people from anywhere in the world.

Barra's leisure industry has experienced an amazing boost and organised kayak tours take place throughout the summer permitting access to coastal features which are difficult if not impossible to reach from land. To the visitor the most obvious change in the attitude to place-names on Barra is no doubt the erection of numerous place-name signs stating the names of villages and townships in Gaelic and English. The recent acknowledgement of Gaelic as one of the official languages of Scotland by the Scottish Executive has helped to strengthen the status of Gaelic on the islands and to ensure at least equal treatment of English and Gaelic. The Ordnance Survey, in the past guilty of rather crude Anglicisation of Gaelic names, has responded with the publication of the new Explorer Series in which the majority of major place-names appear in both English and Gaelic and most names of smaller features in their modern Gaelic spelling.

Acknowledgements:

I am very grateful to Ian A. Fraser for allowing me full access to the place-name material he gathered on Barra in the 1970s and to Arne Kruse for valuable comments on ON in some place-names. I am also indebted to the following contributors of information on place-names and their location mentioned in this article:

D.D. Campbell, Peigi Anna Campbell, Ann MacDonald (Ann Nèill Eoghainn), Ken and Màiri Liz MacKinnon, Michael MacKinnon (Caolas), Ronald MacKinnon (Raogan), Angus MacLean (Ang Mhol), Marion MacLean (Mor Eoin), Mary MacLean (Màiri a Jen), Donald MacNeil (Dogain), Jonathan MacNeil (Eoin a Feannaig), Katie Ann MacNeil (Ceit), Malcolm MacNeil (Calum a Chal), Mary Katherine MacNeil (Catrìona), Neil MacNeil (Neil Handie), Roderick MacNeil (Ruairidh Fhionnlaigh), Christine (Chrissie) and Neil MacPherson (Niall a Chodaidh), Peter Nicholson (Padulla), Donald Patrick Sinclair (Dòmhnaill Phàdraig), Joseph (Jaw) Sinclair and Neil Sinclair (Neilie Mòr).

List of abbreviations

f	feminine
G	Gaelic
m	masculine
n	neuter
ON	Old Norse
OS	Ordnance Survey

Bibliography

Cox, Richard A. V. (1987): *Place-names of the Carloway Registry*, Isle of Lewis, Ph. D. thesis, University of Glasgow, Vol. II, p. 63.

Eysteinnson, Oddgeir (1992): *Norse Settlement-Names of North Harris*, unpublished M.Litt. thesis, University of Aberdeen.

Heggstad, Leiv (1930): *Gamalnorsk ordbok*, Det Norske Samlaget, Oslo.

Maclean manuscripts, University of Edinburgh Library, Special Collection.

MacRae, Farquhar: Maclean manuscripts, P.8103, University of Edinburgh Library, Special Collection.

McDonald, Father Allan (1901-03): "*A list of Non-Gaelic Place-Names in the Island of Mingulay, Near Barra-Head*" as appendix of "*The Norsemen in South Uist Folklore*", Sagabook of the Viking Club, vol. 3, London, pp. 413-433.

Ordnance Survey Object Name Book, Barra Parish, 1878, Scottish Record Office, Edinburgh, RH4/23/106.

Roman Catholic Diocese of Argyll and the Isles Records, 1805/1944, Craigston, Scottish Record Office, Edinburgh, RH21/50/1, 2, 3.

Rygh, Oluf (1898): *Norske Gaardnavne*, Vol. V, Kristiania.

Maps

1823: Maclean "*Map of Barra*" as part of John Thomson, "Southern Part of the Western Isles", scale 1 2/3 miles = 1 inch.

1861-62: Admiralty Chart no. 2770 "*Scotland West Coast, Hebrides, Sound of Barra*", small corrections in 1874, scale 1:15000

1901: Plan of the Estate of Barra belonging to John Gordon of Cluny, surveyor H. Sharbau, RHP 44187, West Register House, Edinburgh.

2003: *Barra & Vatersay / Barraigh agus Bhatarsaigh*, Explorer 452, 1:25 000, Ordnance Survey.

Sound Archive

Flora Boyd, Sound Archive of the School of Scottish Studies, Celtic and Scottish Studies, University of Edinburgh, SA 1974/112/A9.

Malcolm MacAulay, Sound Archive of Celtic and Scottish Studies, School of Literatures, Languages and Cultures, University of Edinburgh, SA1976/9.

Skye

A Hunter-Gatherer Landscape: Searching for Evidence of the Earliest Settlers of the Scottish West Coast

Steven A. Birch

General Background

SCOTLAND is well known for the quality of its surviving archaeological remains. These have attracted the interest of antiquarians and archaeologists from many countries over the years and the evidence of the past continues to inspire survey, excavation and new interpretations. However, when we think of archaeology in Scotland, and the type of sites that continue to inspire and impress, we are constantly reminded of monuments like ruined castles, churches, Atlantic round-houses or Brochs, the large burial cairns and stone circles of the prehistoric period, and the later industrial sites. Archaeological sites of this type are usually visible in the landscape and provide accessible avenues of interpretation, while the investigation of sites rooted in the historic period can sometimes be supplemented by valuable documentary sources. In contrast, searching for the evidence of the earliest settlers of Scotland is a very different proposition.

Evidence for the latter is often very ephemeral in nature and usually comprises a few flakes of chipped stone, a factor that makes the study of the Scottish Mesolithic a rather dull affair for many archaeologists and researchers. In addition, the landscape has changed significantly during the past 10 000 years and studying the Mesolithic hunter-gatherers of Scotland poses an immense challenge. However, for any researcher studying the earliest settlers on these shores, it is this very challenge that inspires research. We can attempt to reconstruct some aspects of Mesolithic life – their technology, their subsistence, their mobility patterns, the manner in which they manipulated their environments, the time of their demise and the rise of Neolithic farming communities.

Nevertheless, before looking at the physical evidence these communities left behind in the archaeological record a survey of the time framework during which these people roamed the Scottish landscape and navigated the seaways is needed to provide a basic picture of the changing environments in which they had to live and adapt. Such criteria are critical in enabling us to search for, and helping to understand the earliest settlement of Scotland.

Setting the Scene: The Ever-Changing Landscape

In order to get closer to the early settlers of the Scottish west coast, and to predict where we may find their habitation sites and how they used the land around them, we must have some understanding of both the past and present landscapes and how they have evolved.

If we go back in time to the last major glaciation of our islands, that of the Devensian between 18 000 and 15 000 years ago, we would find severe arctic conditions with a major ice sheet some one to two kilometres thick covering Scotland (McLeish, 1992:268-69; Smith, 1992:52-53). The Devensian actually began some 110 000 years ago with the ice reaching its maximum extent around 17 000 years ago. The ground free of the ice sheet comprised a tundra landscape and because the oceanic water was locked up in the ice, sea levels were reduced by some 120 metres on those of today. Besides the lowlands of England, Ireland and Wales being free of ice, it is also thought that the North Sea Plain also constituted a major tract of open tundra landscape. Indeed, these North Sea Lowlands may have extended as far north as Shetland (Idem: 53-58).

Compared with the tens of thousands of years during which the climate was deteriorating during the Devensian period, the amelioration was rapid and the British Isles was free of ice within less than 8 000 years. Conditions would still have been harsh for year-round Human settlement at this time with the landscape dominated by open, fairly barren ground, with temperatures still much colder than today. Nevertheless, between 15 000 and 13 000 years ago, with rising temperatures, the northern oceans started to warm and sea levels rose as water was released from the ice. Soils started to accumulate, vegetation developed and animals would have returned to browse with elk, reindeer and giant fallow deer present on the arctic-like grasslands. Human settlement would now have been possible (Wickham-Jones, 1994:32-47).

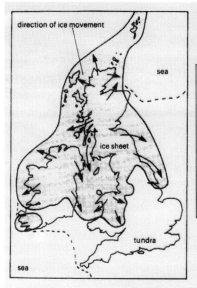

Left – The extent of the Devensian Ice Sheet about 17,000 years ago, showing the general direction of localised ice movements (after McLeish, 1986)

Below – An artist's impression of the relationship between Ice Sheets and Landmass at this stage during the Devensian, showing an open corridor over the North Sea Plain (after Ellery, SNH Publications)

Fig.1: The extent of the Devensian Ice Sheet around 17 000 years ago, including the direction of ice flow and areas interpreted as being free of ice. (After McLeish, 1986 & Ellery, 1996)

However, deglaciation was not constant and was interrupted on several occasions by increases in precipitation associated with movements of the Polar Front, which led to renewed ice accumulation, particularly in Scotland. These events are marked by glacial moraines where the stationary or re-advancing ice sheets left accumulations of eroded debris, many of which can be seen in the Scottish landscape today. The best known event is the 'Loch Lomond Readvance', or Stadial, dated mainly to the period between 11 400 and 10 800 years ago, though ice accumulation may have been under way by 12 000 BP (Roberts, 1998:70-72). Although the main ice sheet at this time was centred on the main mountain mass of central Scotland, smaller ice sheets are known to have been present on the mountains of offshore islands like Skye. In addition, smaller individual corrie glaciers are thought to have been active in Skye in places like the eastern corries of the Trotternish Ridge (Merritt & Stephenson, 2000:16-17). During the 'Loch Lomond Readvance' temperatures dropped once again, the oceans cooled, and tundra conditions would have reshaped the flora and fauna of the area. Birch woodland would have become restricted to locally favourable habitats, to be replaced by open-habitat taxa able to survive on disturbed and seasonally frozen soils. The climate would have been cold and generally dry. It is interesting to speculate what may have happened to the animals and any human populations in western Scotland during this cold snap. The animals would most likely have shifted their grazing to where the vegetation was still accessible, while any people living in the area would have been forced to adjust their lifestyle and movements in association with animal movements. One only has to look at the Arctic environments of more recent times to see how people have adapted to these cold and changeable conditions, and have been able to eke out a living (McGhee, 1996). Also, one can draw some comparisons with the hunter-gatherer communities who inhabited the limestone caves of France and Spain some 18 000 to 12 000 years ago, people who were living to the south of the major ice sheets then covering most of the British landmass. Closer to home, the caves of Cresswell Crags in Derbyshire have produced Upper Palaeolithic material dating back to over 12 000 years ago, while other sites in Kent and Somerset have produced dates of a similar age (Smith, 1992:76-109). These sites, especially the Cresswell caves, would have been virtually on the margin of the ice sheets that spread out to the north.

It is possible that the hunter-gatherers of these Late Glacial times would have made use of plant resources where they could be found. However, existence would not really have been possible for these early settlers without the exploitation of animals. Animals were important not only as sources of food and raw materials but also as competitors. A number, like wolves, bears and foxes, hunted many of the same species as humans and there would also have been competition for accommodation in that wolves and bears also tend to use natural shelters in the landscape. The major animal resources exploited by humans during these Late Glacial periods would have been Mammoth, Woolly Rhino, Bison, Wild Cattle, Horse and Reindeer, with other smaller mammals and birds supplementing the diet. Any hunter-gatherer groups based nearer to the coast would also have exploited the marine biomass, with marine mammals, fish and possibly shellfish playing an important role in sustaining the population (Idem, 1992; Wickham-Jones, 1994).

By around 10 000 years ago, the ice sheets and glaciers that had formed during the 'Loch Lomond Readvance' had all but wasted away and this date is conventionally taken as marking the end of the Devensian, and with it the end of the Pleistocene Epoch. The Holocene Epoch that followed, the period in which we live today, signalled the end of major glacial events and a return to improving climatic conditions. A climatic optimum was reached some 8 500 years ago when Scotland offered an attractive base for year-round human occupation. Post-glacial Scotland provided habitats to support a broad range of animals, while some of the earlier species such as Mammoth, Woolly Rhinoceros and Reindeer, did not survive in these changing environments (Smith, 110-38).

Fig.2: Artist's impression of a coastal hunter-gatherer camp during the Mesolithic (Courtesy of the National Museums & Galleries of Wales.)

The recovery of mean temperature values and increased precipitation provided an improving environment for colonisation by both flora and fauna. Our main source of evidence for the Late-glacial and Post-glacial flora consists of fossil pollen grains from cave deposits, former lake sediments and peat (Edwards & Ralston, 1984 & 1997; Roberts, 1998:29-40). Trees, particularly birch, became increasingly dominant during the ameliorating climate of the Early Holocene and boreal forests were responsible for the initial closing of the landscape. However, the period of the birch forests was relatively short-lived, with mixed deciduous woodland becoming established on the Scottish west coast by around 9000 years ago. These woodlands comprised pine, hazel, oak and elm, although birch remained an important component in this area (Birks, 1973).

The early Post-glacial period would have provided a challenging and ever-changing landscape for the earliest settlers of these lands. The melting of the ice sheets would have produced a land dotted with numerous lakes and melt streams, but as time passed these would have begun to dry out and became progressively overgrown with reed swamp, peat and fen, to be followed by the incoming plants and trees. Other factors would also have had an important impact on the landscape. For example, the melting ice sheets released huge amounts of water back into the oceans sparking a rapid rise in sea level.

These changes in sea level were not constant but proceeded in an irregular fashion. There were periods during which the rising sea levels, or transgressions, were separated by episodes when levels were simply maintained or fell (regressions). The Post-glacial maximum transgression, which occurred some 7 000 years ago in western Scotland, produced sea levels approximately 10 metres above those of today, which resulted in the relatively rapid drowning of significant areas of low-lying land (Smith, 1992:168-80; McLeish, 1992:268-70). The rising sea formed the Straits of Dover, the land bridge between north-east Ireland and south-west Scotland was breached, and the North Sea land bridge was inundated. This resulted in the British Isles becoming isolated from the remainder of mainland Europe at this time.

This sequence of transgressions and regressions which has affected the coasts of the British Isles since the Late-glacial is complex, but for the coasts of western Scotland a further complexity is added by movement of the land relative to the sea. This is known as isostatic recovery or rebound. When the British ice sheet was at its maximum extent and thickness, its enormous weight was sufficient to depress the underlying portions of the earth's crust by an appreciable amount. As the ice melted this pressure and weight was removed and so the surface began to recover and lift.

However, the process of melting and recovery was not simultaneous and recovery of the land surface continued long after the final melting of the ice sheets. Indeed, parts of Scotland are still rising by as much as a few centimetres per century, while those areas further away from the main ice loading centres are gradually sinking below the surface of the sea. The Western and Northern Isles are particularly vulnerable to these latter events. The combined effects of sea level change and isostatic recovery have resulted in many of the raised beaches and other shoreline features, so characteristic of the Scottish west coast, that remain important when considering the locations of possible hunter-gatherer camps of the earliest settlers in the region (Lacaille, 1954:39-45).

Therefore, by around 8 000 years ago, the landscape of western Scotland was a rich and varied one. The woodlands and moorlands would have been home to a wealth of large and small mammal species including red deer, aurochs, bear, wild boar, beaver, hare, marten, otter and fox, while birds would also have been abundant (Smith, 1992). The freshwater lakes and rivers would have been rich in salmonids and other species of fish, while marine resources would have produced sea mammals, fish and shellfish. Archaeological investigations of early settler sites have shown that all of these species would have been exploited during these optimum conditions.

However, these optimum conditions were not static and further change continued throughout the early Holocene. Most of these changes would have been barely discernable throughout the life of an individual, but the combined memory of generations must have revealed constant flux in the landscape. Disappearing coastlands, draining marshland and long-term temperature rises may have been mentally recorded by these people and passed on within a communal memory bank.

Some of these changes must also have been catastrophic in nature, probably on a grand scale, and broadly similar to those experienced throughout the world today. An archaeological site at Castle Street in Inverness, for example, excavated by Wordsworth and found to be of Mesolithic age, showed evidence for inundation by a tidal wave, or 'Tsunami', which was possibly caused by underwater landslips on a massive scale off the Norwegian Banks (Wordsworth, 1985). Evidence for this event has been recognised at other locations in the northeast of Scotland on Mesolithic sites, indicating the devastating scale on which this event took place.

The Early Settlement of Scotland and the development of Hunter-Gatherer Landscape Archaeology

Given the northern latitude and glacial history of Scotland, it is no surprise to learn that there is no unequivocal evidence for Palaeolithic settlement here. However, the Palaeolithic settlement of Britain in general lasted intermittently for some 300 000 years, and though it took place in a generally poor climate, it was also a time of continual environmental change (Wickham-Jones, 1994:32-44). During the warmer interstadials the northern lands would have been suitable for settlement, even if only on a temporary basis. And while the Palaeolithic settlement of England and Wales is well attested, surely the hunting grounds of Scotland would not have been ignored when they were so close to hand.

A few isolated artefacts that might relate to Upper Palaeolithic or Late Glacial activity in Scotland, hand axes and a small number of tanged points (Saville, 1997; Mithen, 2000:9-17), have been recovered from Scotland although the contexts in which they were found remains dubious. Therefore, conventional wisdom has always taught that Scotland was uninhabited until the arrival of the first Mesolithic hunters after the ice age and these finds of potential importance have been generally ignored. However, one site that has caused much debate regarding the early settlement of Scotland is Reindeer Cave, one of the so-called 'bone caves' at Creag nam Uamh, in Sutherland. Excavations at this cave in 1926 recovered over 900 Reindeer antler fragments, along with a possible ivory spear point, possibly suggesting a human presence at the cave in the Upper Palaeolithic (Smith, 1992:160-61; Wickham-Jones, 1994:32-44; Lacaille, 1954:88-90; Lawson, 1981:7-20). Although recent radiocarbon assays carried out on the antler fragments have provided a range of dates covering a period between 44 000 and 22 000 years ago, recent work by archaeologists, geologists and cave morphologists at the site suggests that the antlers may have entered the cave by natural agencies. Therefore, the controversy surrounding this site is set to continue.

Whatever the explanation for the material in Reindeer Cave it is of great significance. Elsewhere in Northern Europe, reindeer was an important resource for the late-glacial hunters and the Sutherland deposits show that there were substantial herds of these animals in the area at this time. However, deposits such as these are a rarity. The cave has clearly protected the material from the dynamic events of later glaciation events and environmental change, and it is only from such a location that we are ever likely to find direct and stratigraphically secure evidence for the late glacial settlement of Scotland.

Before moving on to discuss the evidence we have for the earliest settlement of Scotland along the western seaboard during the Mesolithic, or Middle Stone Age, I would like to briefly discuss how the development of hunter-gatherer landscape archaeology has shaped our understanding of Scotland's past.

When he presented his paper to the Society of Antiquaries of Scotland *A review of the Scottish Mesolithic: a plea for normality*, Peter Woodman painted a rather gloomy picture of the state of Mesolithic research in the region:

> Any assessment of a particular period in Archaeology must be relative, through comparison with its equivalent elsewhere or with other periods of prehistory in the same region. Even if one allows for the fact that there are always problems and biases in recognition, recovery and survival of evidence, it must be admitted that the study of the Mesolithic of Scotland lags behind both the rest of Scotland's prehistory and much of the rest of the European Mesolithic. In fact, in the case of Scotland, it would appear that nature and man have conspired in every possible way to ensure that there was no relatively easy access to information about the Mesolithic. (Woodman, 1989:1)

Although this is a rather bleak picture a renewed interest in Mesolithic studies in Scotland, including a series of new site excavations and landscape-based archaeological projects, are starting to address the underlying problems identified by Woodman.

Early Mesolithic research in Scotland differed very little from work being carried out in other regions of Europe. By the 1920s, a range of clearly comparable stone tool types of a broadly European form were being recognised and were helping to form a typological sequence on which a sound chronology could then be based (Lacaille, 1954). The work undertaken by a number of people contributed to the development of the Scottish 'Mesolithic scene'. These individuals included Peterson, (the Dee Valley, Aberdeenshire), Corrie & Callander (the Tweed Valley sites), Grieve & Anderson (the Oban caves and rock shelters), Bishop (the Oronsay and Risga middens), and Lacaille, who was to contribute so much to the Scottish Mesolithic (Wickham-Jones, 1994:62-5; Mithen, 2000:9-18; Finlayson & Warren, 2000:133). Therefore, it would seem that up until the 1940s, Mesolithic research in Scotland was keeping in touch with new developments in the rest of Europe. However, at some point during the following two decades research on the Scottish Mesolithic became stagnant, with various factors having a dampening effect on further work. Indeed, *The Stone Age of Scotland* (1954) by Lacaille certainly seemed to be the definitive work of the time regarding the Scottish Mesolithic scene, a factor that may have contributed to the fall-off in new research work in the region.

This decline continued until the 1980s and was characterised by a lack of new ideas about how to approach the Scottish Mesolithic. The only obvious exceptions to this general stagnancy can be found in the reports from a number of small-scale excavations. These include: Starr Cottages, Galloway (Affleck, 1986), Auchareoch, Arran (Affleck, *et* al, 1988), Newton on Islay (McCullagh, 1991), the work of John Mercer and Susan Searight on Jura (Mercer 1968, 1970a, 1970b, 1971, 1972, 1974, 1980; Mercer & Searight, 1986; Searight, 1990 & 1993), and John Coles investigation of the site at Morton, Fife (Coles, 1975). While a few long-term projects were about to commence, like the excavation and re-evaluation of the Oronsay middens (Mellars, 1987), and the multi-disciplinary investigation of Farm Fields on the island of Rum (Wickham-Jones, 1990), research into the Scottish Mesolithic was in danger of proceeding on a very selective site by site basis.

A suite of other factors have also had a critical effect on the advancement of Mesolithic research in Scotland and these factors have created a disturbing bias in the record of the colonisation of the region at this time. The identification and interpretation of the Mesolithic record in Scotland is made difficult due to a variety of environmental and economic conditions of the country. Deep blanket peat and blown sand covers much of the landscape and has buried much of the early prehistoric remains. Equally, a substantial portion of the Early Holocene coastline has been lost owing to the highest stand of the maximum transgression, conventionally believed to have lasted until c.6 500 years ago. In addition to these geomorphological factors, which affect the visibility of Mesolithic evidence in Scotland, there are other elements to take into consideration. These include the geographical distribution of population centres within the area, the intensity and dispersion of agriculturally improved ground, the spread of urban developments and the nature and extent of the archaeological fieldwork conducted in the region.

The majority of lithic scatters and potential Mesolithic sites found in Scotland seem to derive from a few specific sources. The amateur archaeologist and collector has without doubt made the greatest contribution to the basic

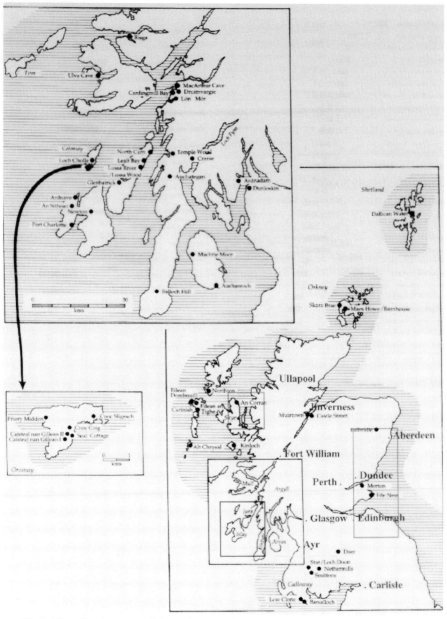

Fig.3: Map showing some of the major sites discussed in the text and areas of Scotland covered by larger landscape-based surveys. (After Mithen, 2000 & Birch, 2003.)

substructure of Mesolithic research, with many collections of artefacts deposited with local museums or still held in private hands. These amateur archaeologists often have links to local field clubs, archaeological societies and trusts, and museums, while more recently they have forged links with the larger university and research-based projects. Individuals who have played an important role in advancing the development of Mesolithic research in Scotland include John Mercer, who carried out extensive fieldwork on the island of Jura, Tom Affleck, who carried out fieldwork both in the southwest of Scotland and on the island of Arran, and Frank Newall, who recorded several new Mesolithic flint scatters on Islay (Mithen, 2000:23-5). Although principally amateurs in their field, these archaeologists published their findings within the wider public domain, a feature that has been lacking at times within the professional field. A significant proportion of the fieldwork carried out by these amateur archaeologists has now been incorporated or used as base-line data within the recent multi-disciplinary research-based projects that have taken place in Scotland.

During the later stages of the 1980s and into the turn of the new Millennium, the nature of Scottish Mesolithic studies has changed dramatically. Sites like Farm Fields on Rum (Wickham-Jones, 1990), Newton on Islay (McCullagh, 1989), Ulva Cave on Mull (Bonsall *et* al, 1991, 1992 & 1994) and Fife Ness (Wickham-Jones & Dalland, 1998), have been excavated and published. We have also witnessed the formation of larger-scale multi-disciplinary research-based projects looking at the study of hunter-gatherer archaeology on a landscape-based scale. The ten years of research, survey and excavation work undertaken as a part of the *Southern Hebrides Mesolithic Project* (Mithen, 2000) has just been published, and in a way replicates the impact of Lacaille's *Stone Age of Scotland* (Lacaille, 1954) some fifty years ago. The quality and breadth of fieldwork and post-excavation analysis, and the overall impact of the publication itself will now set the standard to which all future work will be judged and compared. Hopefully, the publication of this work will not hold back the advances being made in Scottish Mesolithic studies.

Following in the shadow of the *Southern Hebrides* work is the *Scotland's First Settlers Project*, based firmly within the northern region of the Hebrides. This project is now progressing into its fifth and final year of fieldwork and publication should be forthcoming in the near future. There are also further Mesolithic landscape projects concentrating on the major eastern river systems of Scotland such as the Tweed, Lunan and Ythan (Finlayson & Warren, 2000). Some archaeologists have brought a fresh approach to Mesolithic studies in

Scotland. Graeme Warren, based at the University of Edinburgh, is attempting to address the more complex intellectual, social and economic issues surrounding the Mesolithic within a landscape perspective. Most of his fieldwork has been undertaken around the east-coast of Scotland and along the major river valleys that penetrate the hinterland. He has also introduced the dimension of 'Mesolithic Seascapes', where he presents a focus on the interaction between the skilled practice of sailing and the environment, seascape perception and potential maritime lore and knowledge amongst the foraging communities of the maritime west coast (Warren, 2000).

Tony Pollard of Glasgow University has also taken the study of the Mesolithic Period in Scotland to new dimensions, searching for evidence of these communities beyond the flints and lithic scatters that pervade the pages of most journals and reports specialising on this subject (Pollard, 1996). Like Warren, he has also attempted to discuss the motives which may have drawn Mesolithic people to the small islands of the western seaboard of Scotland and has undertaken a significant core of research relating to potential Mesolithic burial rites and the exploitation of marine resources in Scotland.

Therefore, the following ten or twenty years should witness a wealth of new fieldwork and published data relating to the post-glacial settlement of Scotland. This fieldwork combined with advances in archaeological methodology is already amending the earliest dates for this settlement phase with inland sites such as Daer 1 in the Lowther Hills, Clydesdale, producing a radiocarbon date of 9075+/-80 BP (Mithen, 2000:20-21). However, the recent discovery of a small lithic assemblage and burnt hazelnut shells has provided dates for the earliest known remains of human settlement in Scotland.

The site, found by a team of amateur archaeologists from the Edinburgh Archaeological Field Society, was uncovered during the excavation of a Roman settlement at Crammond, near Edinburgh, and has produced radiocarbon dates ranging between 8 600 and 8 200 BC (Saville, *pers comm.*). The site also provides the earliest date in Britain for the 'geometric' style of microlith tool manufacture, an advanced style traditionally regarded as a Late Mesolithic development, not found in England before 7 800 BC. This information raises intriguing questions regarding the origin and spread of this new stone tool technology, while the age of the site in general will open a discussion about the early post-glacial climate in Scotland and when it became suitable for permanent habitation.

Prospecting for new Mesolithic sites and my Integration into the Scotland's First Settlers Project

By Autumn 1998, I had gained valuable experience in the field of landscape archaeology and my studies and research into the prehistory of Scotland had provided a general framework for the early settlement record of the region, particularly for the Mesolithic/Neolithic transition and its wider implications within Scotland. Fieldwork in the Skye and Lochalsh area had resulted in the discovery of several lithic scatters and rock shelter sites with associated midden deposits. These sites were recorded and I also collected any potentially diagnostic artefactual material eroding from them. This included a number of sites close to my home on the island of Scalpay, Skye, mainly scatters of struck stone centred on eroding animal tracks on the surface of raised beach platforms. Casual surveys of this ground in the past had failed to find such sites and this shows the importance of the amateur within his home territory. By looking at the same erosion features over a prolonged period of time and differing weather conditions, I was able to detect five distinct lithic scatters in the area. These sites would be included in the *Scotland's First Settlers* Project database for future investigation and analysis.

The evidence for the earliest settlement of the Skye and Lochalsh area at this time was fairly sparse. However, the work of Pollard on the Ardnamurchan Peninsula, particularly the re-assessment of the open midden site on the island of Risga, Sunart (Pollard *et al*, 1996), and the large-scale excavations of Wickham-Jones on Rum (Wickham-Jones, 1990), had already indicated the potential for Mesolithic settlement. The lithic scatter found at Redpoint, Outer Loch Torridon, Wester Ross, by fellows of the Society of Antiquaries and re-visited later by A.F. Gray during 1954 and 1956, had produced stone tools to suggest a Mesolithic presence there (Gray, 1960). While to the south of Redpoint, 'rescue' excavations by Micheal Walker at Shieldaig revealed a microlithic assemblage of stone tools and a limited amount of organic material. Radiocarbon determinations for the organic material, mainly on fragments of charred wood and a wooden implement, provided dates ranging between 2230+/- 540 BC and 2650+/- 160 BC (Walker, 1973). Unfortunately, the final results of Walkers work at Shieldaig remain unpublished and the context from which the C14 samples were obtained remains dubious.

However, the most significant Mesolithic site discovered in the Skye and Lochalsh area at this time was the rock shelter at An Corran, near Staffin, Skye.

Initially identified by Martin Wildgoose during fieldwork in the area in 1988, salvage excavations were carried out at the site during December 1993 and January 1994, in advance of rock blasting for road works (Saville & Miket, 1994). Unfortunately, although the archaeological deposits remaining at the site after the excavation were protected by a covering of Teram and rock armour fill, most of the cliff face including the shelter was eventually destroyed. Although the excavation of the rock shelter at An Corran only removed around one-fifth of the in-situ archaeological deposits, it produced a substantial assemblage of stone tools and well preserved bone artefacts. The quality of the organic remains on site was due to several important factors, including the presence of midden deposits (including marine shellfish, fish and animal remains) sealed below a layer of wind-blown sand. Radiocarbon determinations on bone artefacts from the site produced dates ranging between 7590+/-90BP and 3885+/-65BP, indicating the prolonged use of the shelter through time.

Therefore, except for the Mesolithic sites of An Corran, Shieldaig and Redpoint (although the latter two sites have provided Mesolithic artefacts, but

Fig.4: Aerial view of the excavations carried out at the Sand rock shelter by the Scotland's First Settlers Project in April/May 2000. The shell midden is indicated by the light-coloured area in the image, where the two trenches meet (after Birch, 2002)

no Mesolithic dates), the landscape seemed to be devoid of further evidence for settlement during this early prehistoric phase. However, it would seem rather that this situation was a result of the geomorphology of the area and a general lack of fieldwork, rather than an absence of a Mesolithic presence. Of the three new rock shelter and midden sites discovered by the close of 1998, two of these, Loch a' Sguirr on Raasay and Sand at Applecross, had produced unstratified artefacts which seemed to fit a Mesolithic typology. Trial excavations at these sites would later prove these initial interpretations.

The Scotland's First Settlers Project (SFS Project) was initially brought to my attention during the autumn of 1998. The Project Directors, Dr. Bill Finlayson, Dr. Karen Hardy and Caroline Wickham-Jones (Bill Finlayson left the project during 2000 to take up an archaeological post in Jordan) contacted me through Martin Wildgoose, who had already agreed to assist with the fieldwork aspects of the project. The Project was designed as a small-scale regional study of the area of the Inner Sound, a large expanse of water enclosed by the east coast of Skye and the western shore of the adjacent Scottish Mainland. The principal chronological focus of the project is the Mesolithic and the earliest evidence of the Neolithic, while still recognising more recent developments, which display cultural and economic continuity.

Fig.5: Excavations at the Early Mesolithic site at Camas Daraich,
in the south of Skye, during 2000 (Birch, 2000)

Having contacted me at this early stage in the project, I produced for the Directors results of my fieldwork at the new rock shelter sites. Along with the already known Mesolithic sites identified within the project area, these would provide the primary focus for the 1999 fieldwork season and were included in the Project's Research Design. Therefore, test-pit excavations of the rock shelters of Crowlin, Loch a' Sguirr and Sand 1, ran concurrently with a large block of coastal survey, which was designed to identify and record new potential sites in the area.

The results of the first season of fieldwork were published within the Data Structure Report (Finalyson *et al*, 1999). Radiocarbon determinations from two of the three rock shelter sites, Loch a' Sguirr and Sand 1, produced Mesolithic dates; while the most impressive shelter of the three, on the Crowlin Islands, produced a range of dates starting within the Iron Age. The quality of the sites and the artefactual material they produced had provided the necessary impetus and encouragement to take the project forward, while the coastal survey had identified a significant number of new sites for inclusion in the database. With these initially exciting results, the Project Directors secured the necessary funding for the 2000, 2001 and 2002 field seasons (Hardy & Wickham-Jones, 2000, 2001 and 2002). The aims and objectives were to continue with the coastal survey, which would include the remaining sections of the east coast of the island of Skye, the adjacent Mainland coastline between Kyle of Lochalsh and Red Point, Outer Loch Torridon, and the offshore islands within the Inner Sound basin. In addition to this work, the Sand 1 rock shelter was targeted for more detailed investigations including a major excavation during the months of April and May 2000.

Designed to run alongside these various avenues of investigation within the project, a team of archaeologists would follow in the wake of the coastal survey to test-pit new sites, and to carry out a series of shovel-pitting surveys. The latter strategy was designed to sample four distinct areas of raised beach platform, in order to assess the possible distribution of sites within the landscape that were not detectable within the usual coastal survey parameters. In addition, fieldwork was carried out by Robert Shiel and Andrew Stewart to gather evidence regarding the environment of the Applecross Peninsula, while Mike Cressey completed a series of shovel-pit transects around the Sand site and a reconnaissance around Sand Bay, to determine the geomorphology of the area.

The Sand rock shelter site was excavated using an open area strategy, which covered a section of the midden deposits and an adjacent area of terrace

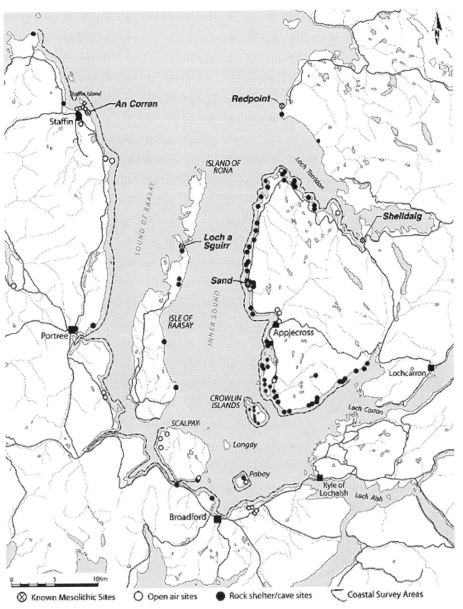

Fig.6: Map of the Inner Sound showing the distribution of archaeological sites identified during fieldwork in 1999/2000 by the Scotland's First Settlers Project. *(After Hardy & Wickham-Jones, 2000.)*

to north and east. The excavation work identified the extent of a discrete organic midden deposit dating to the early Mesolithic period, overlying further archaeological remains in the form of bone and antler waste as well as lithic material. Though detailed post-excavation work has yet to be completed, it is clear that the Sand site has much to offer in assisting our interpretation and understanding of the Scottish Mesolithic and later prehistoric periods (Hardy & Wickham-Jones, 2003). A wealth of new sites were also identified and test-pitted during the coastal survey phase, several of these producing artefacts of possible Mesolithic age, while the excavation of the Sand rock shelter produced some important archaeological finds and a wide-range of faunal remains. However, the most surprising information to derive from the excavation at Sand was the radiocarbon dates, the earliest C14 date from Sand (8 470 years BP) making the rock shelter there the most northerly settlement site of this period in Scotland.

One particular site of some potential and significance found during the SFS survey was the inter-tidal peat deposits and tree remains at Clachan Old Harbour, on the island of Raasay. The site on Raasay when first identified were exposed over an area of approximately 3500 square metres, the rafts of peat, tree boles and trunks being interspersed with more recent marine deposits (sand and shingle). Small stands of seaweed tend to obscure the remains of this eroding ancient ground surface and it is only accessible during the low tide. The site was surveyed during a later visit and a detailed plan was drawn of some of the better-preserved tree remains. It was during this visit that we discovered a single flake of baked mudstone attached to a tree root, while a second lithic (a weathered piece of Rum Bloodstone) was located in close proximity within surface shingle deposits. The combination of ancient forest and ground surface, and the two struck lithics, caused some excitement with the prospects of a prehistoric site nearby.

Inter-tidal sites of this type are quite rare in the Inner Hebrides and can provide a wealth of information relating to vegetation sequences through time, including their associated radiocarbon dates (for example see Edwards, 2000). However, the geomorphology of the surrounding area can also be investigated, especially with regard to fluctuations in sea level (eustatic rise and fall) and isostatic uplifting of the land after the retreat of the last Ice Age (Dawson & Dawson, 2000). Having discussed and stressed the importance of the Clachan site with the Project Directors we have recently returned for a third visit, along with Prof. Kevin Edwards from the University of Aberdeen's Geography Department, to collect environmental samples. Core samples of the peat and the associated marine deposits were taken, along with wood samples for species identification. Initial results from the work at Clachan Harbour suggest the presence of woodland in the area some 9100 years ago, with birch the predominant tree species. However, the presence of hazelnut shells also implies hazel was present within the mixed deciduous woodland (Green, *pers comm.*).

So far, the SFS Project has demonstrated the survival of a remarkable density of sites around the Inner Sound, although we cannot be certain as yet how many of these sites indicate a Mesolithic presence. The marine topography, with its numerous islands, no doubt facilitated travel and settlement, both of which are central to the nomadic hunter-gatherer way of life, as envisaged for the Scottish Mesolithic. A certain aspect of this travel through the landscape is represented by the different stone raw materials, procured for manufacturing stone tools. Recent work carried out around the Staffin Bay area on Skye and on the island of Rum, has identified possible extraction sites for these raw materials (Hardy & Wickham-Jones, 2000, 2001 and 2002; Birch, 2002).

Many of the lithic scatter sites identified and recorded during SFS fieldwork contain Rum Bloodstone, the source of which has been known for some time on the flanks of Bloodstone Hill on the island of Rum. This distinctive stone, derived from volcanic sources, must have had some form of special attraction for the early stone-age communities of the Scottish west coast, and was later mined for the manufacture of jewellery during the later stages of the nineteenth century. The material is not particularly well suited to knapping and the manufacture of stone tools, although it has a reasonably good conchoidal fracture. However, this material has been recovered from Mesolithic sites some sixty to seventy km away from Rum, indicating some special significance for the material.

Additional sites of Mesolithic date have also been located in areas bordering the SFS Project area, such as those at Camas Daraich at the Point of Sleat, on Skye (Wickham-Jones & Hardy, 2000), and Rudh an Dunain Cave, near to Glen Brittle on Skye (Scott, 1934). For a people dependant on local resources for their survival, the Inner Sound and the Scottish west coast in general would have provided an excellent environment.

The topography provided a rich resource base from which various niches could be exploited, including salt and freshwater, shallow and deep water, coastal, lowland and upland habitats. This type of resource base would fit well with the traditional view of the Scottish Mesolithic, one of mobility, especially within the fluid seascape of the west coast.

The SFS Project has identified a number of Mesolithic sites in the area which all have dates ranging between the seventh to the sixth millennia BC. Although it is not yet possible to relate one site directly to another, they all appear to be linked by various aspects of the material culture. The Project has noted close similarities in the types of tools found at the sites, as well as the types of raw materials exploited from which to manufacture the stone tools. The Project has also confirmed the existence of a well-established Mesolithic presence further north in Scotland than previously thought, although since the start of the project, new Mesolithic sites have been located in Caithness (Humphreys, *pers comm.*).

However, as more sites are found, so the picture of Mesolithic settlement on the Scottish west coast becomes more complex. The precise date of the initial colonization of Scotland after the end of the last glaciation may never be known, but our picture of the Mesolithic in Scotland has changed dramatically in the last couple of decades. The SFS Project is contributing significantly to this changing picture with general interpretations regarding raw material source areas and their influence on early settlement patterns; material culture, mobility, and economic interpretation; changes with time and assimilation or isolation as the Neolithic took hold in the area. But, while some interpretations can be put forward regarding the Mesolithic settlement of the west coast of Scotland, the work of the SFS Project has opened up other areas of study. What were the attractions of this area during the early Holocene? How far did people range? What were the bases for the necessities of life? How was the area affected by contemporary climate change and how did its inhabitants cope with this? The work of the Project, combined with the fieldwork undertaken on the Scottish west coast during the past 20 years, is starting to address these questions, helping us to get closer to the hunter-gatherer's of the Scottish Mesolithic.

References

Affleck, T.L. (1986) *Excavations at Starr, Loch Doon 1985.* Glasgow Archaeological Society Bulletin 22, 14-21.

Affleck, T.L., Edwards, K.J. & Clarke, A. (1988) *Archaeological and palynological studies at the Mesolithic pitchstone and flint site of Auchareoch, Isle of Arran.* Proc. Soc. Antiq. Scot., 118, 37-59.

Birch, S.A. (2002) *Scotland's First Settlers: The involvement and contribution of an Independent Archaeologist within a multi-disciplinary research project.* Unpublished Portfolio, University of Aberdeen.

Birks, H.J.B. (1973) *Past and Present Vegetation of the Isle of Skye: A Palaeoecological Study*. Cambridge University Press.

Bonsall, C., Sutherland, D.G. & Lawson, T.J. (1991) *Excavation in Ulva Cave, western Scotland 1989: a preliminary report*. Mesolithic Miscellany 12 (2), 18-23.

Bonsall, C., Sutherland, D.G., Lawson, T.J. & Russell, N. (1992) *Excavation in Ulva Cave, western Scotland 1989: a preliminary report*. Mesolithic Miscellany 13 (1), 7-13.

Bonsall, C., Sutherland, D.G., Russell, N., Coles, G., Paul, C.R.C., Huntley, J.P. & Lawson, T.J. (1994) *Excavation in Ulva Cave, western Scotland 1990-91: a preliminary report*. Mesolithic Miscellany 15 (1), 8-21.

Coles, J. (1971) *The early settlement of Scotland: excavation at Morton, Fife*. Proceedings of the Prehistoric Society 37, 284-366.

Dawson, S. & Dawson, A. (2000) *Late Pleistocene and Holocene Relative Sea Level Changes in Gruinart, Islay*. In Mithen, S. (ed.) *Hunter-gatherer landscape archaeology* (see below), pp.99-113.

Edwards, K.J. & Ralston, I. (1984) *Postglacial hunter-gatherers and vegetational history in Scotland*. Proc. Soc. Antiq. Scot., 114, 15-34.

Edwards, K.J. & Ralston, I. Eds. (1997) *Scotland: Environment and Archaeology, 8000 BC-AD 1000*. Chichester: John Wiley & Sons.

Edwards, K.J. (2000) *Vegetation History of the Southern Inner Hebrides during the Mesolithic Period*. In Mithen, S. (ed.) *Hunter-gatherer landscape archaeology* (see below), pp.115-27.

Finlayson, B., Hardy, K. & Wickham-Jones, C.R. (1999) *Scotland's First Settlers: Data Structure Report 1999*. Centre for Field Archaeology, University of Edinburgh.

Finlayson, B. & Warren, G. (2000) *The Mesolithic of Eastern Scotland*. In Young, R. (ed) *Mesolithic Lifeways: Current Research from Britain and Ireland*, pp.133-42. Leicester Archaeology Monographs No.7.

Gray, A.F. (1960) *'A collection of stone artefacts from Redpoint, Loch Torridon, Ross-shire'*. Proc. Soc. Antiq. Scot., 93, 236-37.

Hardy, K. & Wickham-Jones, C.R. (2000) *Scotland's First Settlers: Data Structure Report 2000*. Centre for Field Archaeology, University of Edinburgh.

Hardy, K. & Wickham-Jones, C.R. (2001) *Scotland's First Settlers: Data Structure Report 2001*. Department of Archaeology, University of Edinburgh.

Hardy, K. & Wickham-Jones, C.R. (2002) *Scotland's First Settlers: Project Work and Sea Loch Survey 2002 – Data Structure Report*.

Hardy, K. & Wickham-Jones, C.R. (2003) *Scotland's First Settlers: An Investigation into Settlement, Territoriality and Mobility during the Mesolithic in the Inner Sound*. In Larsson, L. *et al* (eds.) *Mesolithic on the Move: Proceedings of the Meso 2000 Conference*. Oxbow Books, Oxford, pp.369-81.

Lacaille, A.D. (1954) *The Stone Age in Scotland*. Oxford University Press.

Lawson, T.J. (1981) *The 1926-7 excavations of the Creag nan Uamh Bone Caves, near Inchnadamph, Sutherland*. Proc. Soc. Antiq. Scot., 111, 7-20.

Lees, G. & Duncan, K. (1996) *Coasts: Scotland's Living Landscapes*. Scottish Natural Heritage Publications.

McCullagh, R. (1991) *Excavation at Newton, Islay*. Glasgow Archaeological Journal 15, 23-52).

McGhee, R. (1996) *Ancient People of the Arctic*. UBC Press.

McLeish, A. (1992) *Geological Science*. Nelson

Mellars, P.A. ed. (1987) *Excavations on Oronsay: Prehistoric Human Ecology on a Small Island*. Edinburgh University Press.

Mercer, J. (1968) *Stone tools from a washing-limit deposit of the highest Post-Glacial transgression, Lealt Bay, Isle of Jura*. Proc. Soc. Antiq. Scot., 100, 1-46.

Mercer, J. (1970a) *Flint tools from the present tidal zone, Lussa Bay, Isle of Jura, Argyll*. Proc. Soc. Antiq. Scot., 102, 1-30.

Mercer, J. (1970b) *The microlithic succession in northern Jura, Argyll, Western Scotland*. Quarternaria 13, 177-83.

Mercer, J. (1971) *A regression time stone workers camp 33ft O.D. Lussa River, Isle of Jura*. Proc. Soc. Antiq. Scot., 103, 1-32.

Mercer, J. (1972) *Microlithic and Bronze Age camps 75-26ft O.D. N. Carn, Isle of Jura*. Proc. Soc. Antiq. Scot., 104, 1-22.

Mercer, J. (1974) *Glenbatrick waterhole, a microlithic site on the Isle of Jura*. Proc. Soc. Antiq. Scot., 105, 9-32.

Mercer, J. (1980) *Lussa Wood I: the late glacial and early postglacial occupation of Jura*. Proc. Soc. Antiq. Scot., 110, 1-31.

Mercer, J. & Searight, S. (1986) *Glengarrisdale: confirmation of Jura's third microlithic phase*. Proc. Soc. Antiq. Scot., 116, 41-55.

Merritt, J. & Stephenson, D. (2000) *Skye: a landscape fashioned by geology*. Scottish Natural Heritage/British Geological Survey.

Mithen, S. (2000) *Hunter-gatherer landscape archaeology: The Southern Hebrides Mesolithic Project 1988-98*. Vol.1 – McDonald Institute Monographs.

Pollard, T. (1996) *Coastal Environments, Cosmology and Ritual Practice in Early Prehistoric Scotland*. In Pollard, T. & Morrison, A. (eds) *The Early Prehistory of Scotland*, pp.198-210. Edinburgh University Press.

Pollard, T., Atkinson, J. & Banks, I. (1996) *It is the technical side of the work which is my stumbling block: a shell midden site on Risga reconsidered*. In Pollard, T. & Morrison, A. (eds) *The Early Prehistory of Scotland*, pp.165-82. Edinburgh University Press.

Roberts, N. (1998) *The Holocene: An Environmental History*. Blackwell.

Saville, A. (1997) *Palaeolithic Handaxes in Scotland*. Proc. Soc. Antiq. Scot. 127, 1-16.

Saville, A. & Miket, R. (1994) *An Corran rockshelter: a major new Mesolithic site*. Past 18, December 1994, 9-10.

Scott, W.L. (1934) *'Excavations of Rudh an Dunain Cave, Skye'*. Proc. Soc. Antiq. Scot., 68, 200-23.

Searight, S. (1990) *Mesolithic activity at Carn southern raised beach, Isle of Jura*. Proc. Soc. Antiq. Scot., 120, 7-16.

Searight, S. (1993) *Lussa Bay, Isle of Jura, Argyll: a note on additional tools*. Proc. Soc. Antiq. Scot., 123, 1-8.

Smith, C. (1992) *Late Stone Age Hunters of the British Isles*. Routledge.

Walker, M. (1973) *Archaeological excavation of a microlithic assemblage at Shieldaig, Wester Ross, Scotland*. Unpublished Preliminary Report.

Warren, G. (2000) *Seascapes: People, boats and inhabiting the Later Mesolithic in Western Scotland*. In Young, R. (ed) *Mesolithic Lifeways: Current Research from Britain and Ireland*. Leicester Archaeology Monographs No.7, pp.97-104.

Wickham-Jones, C.R. (1990) *Rhum: Mesolithic and Later Sites at Kinloch: Excavations 1984-1986*. (Monograph Series 7) Edinburgh: Society of Antiquaries of Scotland.

Wickham-Jones, C.R. (1994) *Scotland's First Settlers*. Historic Scotland/Batsford.

Wickham-Jones, C.R. & Hardy, K. (2000) *Camas Daraich 2000: Data Structure Report*. Department of Archaeology, University of Edinburgh.

Woodman, P.C. (1989) *A review of the Scottish Mesolithic: a plea for normality!* Proc. Soc. Antiq. Scot., 119, 1-32.

Wordsworth, J. (1985) *The excavation of a Mesolithic horizon at 13-24 Castle Street, Inverness*. Proc. Soc. Antiq Scot., 115, 89-103.

Skye from Somerled to A.D. 1500

G.W.S. Barrow

THE bigger islands of western Scotland may be, and no doubt have been, classified in various ways. From the standpoint of the historian of medieval Scotland one particularly helpful classification is by language and culture — with the all-important proviso that neither of these features possesses an accepted, self-evident chronology, and for the historian chronology is fundamental. From the geography of Ptolemy of Alexandria, in the second century after Christ, we can deduce that the Big Four, among the islands outwith the Kintyre Peninsula — i.e., omitting Arran — were Lewis, Skye, Mull and Islay (Watson, 1926:6 and at 37-42; Richmond, 1954:134 and at 136). Two of these already had names close to those we recognise today, Skitis and Malaios. We must envisage a northern British, Brittonic-speaking population spread, rather thinly, across the isles. If, taking a hint from Adamnán (Sharpe, 1995:136-37 and at 293-95),[1] we call them Picts[2] we shall not be led astray, provided that we allow some cultural differences between society in Skye and those in the rich firthlands of Easter Ross or the relatively rich plain of Strathmore (Sutherland, 1997:72-73).[3]

Between the time of Columba in the sixth century and the time of Somerled in the twelfth Skye must have experienced two major social and cultural revolutions. Between the end of the sixth century and the end of the eighth the Pictish or north Brittonic language — of which traces have been left just across the water from here, in Applecross, at Pitalman (Pitalmit, Bailanailm)

---

1 In the earlier edition of A.O. and M.O. Anderson, rev. M.O. Anderson (1991:62-3)

2 Adamnán reports that Columba needed an interpreter to preach the gospel to Artbranan.

3 This book provides a convenient comparison of Pictish stone carving in Skye and Raasay with that in Easter Ross and Strathmore.

in Glenelg and Pitnean in Lochcarron (Watson, 1926:78 and at 458)[4] — must have given way to the Q-Celtic Old Irish language already in general use in Argyll and perhaps as far north as Ardnamurchan. A language switch on this scale must imply substantial immigration as well as assimilation. Despite the presence of *na h'Annaidean* in Barvas (Watson, 1926:253),[5] there seems no compelling reason to believe that this northward push of Gaelic speakers reached further than Harris, if indeed as far (Bannatyne Club, 1851-55, ii:377-78);[6] but where Skye is concerned the push must have been effective and thoroughgoing. Dr Barbara Crawford has written that 'there appears to be a general consensus among place-name specialists that none of the Celtic place-names in the Western Isles can be proved to be of pre-Norse origin, and as far as Lewis is concerned ''most or all non-Norse names have a post-Norse character''' (Crawford, 1987:96). There seem to be two insuperable difficulties here. For one thing, if we take the term 'Western Isles' literally, it surely cannot be maintained that islands such as Islay, Jura and Mull have no Gaelic place-names of pre-Norse date.[7] Even if Dr Crawford's 'Western Isles' means the Outer Isles, it is hard to accept that Kilbarr of Barra is post-Norse — my money would be on an unrecorded *Innis-bharr* preceding Barrey, for Barra. For another thing, we must consider the church establishments of Skye. Dedications to Mary, in Sleat (Bannatyne Club, 1851-55, ii, I:340),[8] in Duirinish (ibid:359),[9] on

---

4   Watson, *CPNS*, 407 deals with the rare place-names containing Pictish *pett*, 'portion, share', to be found in Lochcarron (Pitnean, now obsolete) and Glenelg. Watson was, I believe, wrong to refer to two distinct *pett-* place-names in Glenelg. There seems in fact to have been only one, first recorded as Petalman [*RMS*, iii, no.2297] later as Pitchalman [*Retours*, Inverness, no.19] eventually, as Bailanailm, the form appearing on the earliest O.S. 6 inch map [Inverness-shire, 1876, Sheet XLVIII]. Pitalmit is shown on the map of Inverness-shire by William Johnson published by J. Thomson (Edinburgh, 1830). I am grateful to Dr Virginia Glenn for introducing me to this map.

5   I cannot find the name on modern maps.

6   The old church of Harris was called Kilbride, and on the small island of Killegray in the Sound of Harris there were Teampull and Tobar na h'Annaid. These names point to some antiquity.

7   For example, in Islay, Loch Finlaggan, Dùn Guaidhre; in Jura Beinn an Oir, Loch Tairbeart; in Mull Beinn Mhór (Ben More) seem unlikely to be of post-Norse date.

8   Kilmore (NG 658069).

9   Kilmuir (NG 256477)

the west side of Trotternish (ibid:349),[10] and to Christ in Strathsuardal near Broadford (ibid:343-44),[11] might of course have been brought in by newly-converted Norse men and women. But it is not seriously conceivable that the thoroughgoing provision of dedicated Christian worship sites right across Skye is to be dated later than the Norse settlements. In Trotternish and Raasay we have Kilmalúag,[12] in Minginish Kilmolruy,[13] in Snizort Kilcholmkill,[14] in Glendale Kilchoan,[15] at Portree Kiltalorcan,[16] in Lyndale Kildonan[17] and in Vaternish and Uig *cill-Chonnáin*, Saint Connán's church.[18] Columcille, Donnán, Molúoc, Connán, Talorcan and Maelrubha were not the saints of converted Norsemen; nor was this name-construction characteristic of the period after *c*.850. Talorcan, in particular, is a very obscure saint, seemingly a Pict from his name, otherwise known only as patron of Kiltarlity west of Inverness, of Fordyce near Cullen and of Logie Buchan near Ellon (Watson, 1926:298). And why, or for that matter how, did the notably early element *annaid* (< *antiquitatem*, 'superior church') come to be established in Skye, as for example

---

10 Kilmuir (NG 3870).

11 Cill Chriosd (NG 616207)

12 NG 436748 (Kilmalúag of Trotternish); NG 547367 (Kilmalúog of Raasay).

13 NG 375260 (Kilmolruy of Minginish).

14 NG 418486 (shown as 'Chapel').

15 The remains of a 'Roman Catholic' chapel in Glendale, reported on in 1790 [*OSA*, xx, 163-64], presumably represented the medieval church of Kilchoan. I have not located this church, the graveyard of which is mentioned in [Nicolson, *History of Skye*, 282].

16 The name Kiltalorcan is not on modern maps, but the site of the church seems to be at NG 497443, marked 'Chapel' in Gothic. For the church and its dedication see [Mackinlay, *Ancient church Dedications in Scotland: non-scriptural dedications*, 213; Watson, *CPNS*, 298; *OPS*, ii, I, 355 'Ceilltarraglan' (misinterpreted)].

17 NG 3554 (no church site is marked on the 1:50000 O.S. map).

18 NG 225613 (Trumpan church, with medieval carved burial stone in the graveyard); NG 4063 (Uig of Trotternish, for whose dedication to St Connán [Watson, *CPNS*, 282; Dunlop and Cowan, *CSSR*, 19 and at 26].

Clach na h-Annaide and Tobar na h-Annaide at Kilbride near Torrin, west of Kilcrist? There is also Annait in Vaternish. *Annaid* is surely an emphatically pre-Norse term (Watson, 1926:250-54).[19]

By the mid-ninth century or even earlier the second major social and cultural revolution to affect Skye must have been well under way. This of course was the Norse settlement, which must surely have been as thoroughgoing in Skye as in Lewis and Islay, more thoroughgoing than in Mull or Arran. As the overwhelming majority of surviving old settlement names in Skye are of Norse origin, we cannot underestimate the thoroughness of the Norwegian occupation of the island, beginning perhaps in the earlier ninth century. But the point must not be pushed too far. Although the Ptolemaic name for Lewis, Dumna, disappeared, the Ptolemaic names for Skye (Skitis) and Mull (Malaios) survived and Islay (Ile) is an old name. The Norse invaders did not change these names, any more than they changed Bute, Arran, Rathlin or Kintyre. In Skye they can surely not have eliminated the existing population, although they may have enslaved many of them. The lineage and family of Somerled bear witness to miscegenation and assimilation. Sumarliði itself is Norse, but while his father Gillebrigte and his grandfather Gilleadhamhnán bore Gaelic names, Somerled gave Norse names to his younger sons Raonull (Raghnall) and Olaf while the name of his eldest, Dubhgall (literally 'black foreigner' or Dane), points to a Scandinavian link (Duncan and Brown, 1956-57:192-220).[20]

'Skye from Somerled to 1500' presents us with a long span of history which in principle ought to be crammed to bursting-point with events. For a variety of reasons, however, we lack the evidence for a continuous history of Skye. The division of the isles which followed the great sea battle off Colonsay (January 1156), in which neither Somerled nor his opponent Godfrey II son of Olaf the Red king of Man could claim victory (Anderson, 1922, ii:231-32;

---

19 Despite the arguments deployed by Clancy [Clancy, 'Annat in Scotland and the origins of the parish', 91-115], that the term *annaid* (Olr, *andóit*) in Scotland indicates a church in a superior relationship to others, i.e. a potential 'parish church', a post-Norse date for this term seems unlikely.

20 See also Sellar [Sellar, 'The origins and ancestry of Somerled', 123-34]. Although Mr Sellar makes a strong case for the reliability of Somerled's pedigree over eight generations back to Godfrey son of Fergus he agrees that Godfrey's name points to intermarriage between Norse and Gaelic elements occurring remarkably early.

Broderick, 1979:f.37v.), left Skye outwith the area which generated most narrative and record sources until after the Treaty of Perth in 1266 (Duncan and Brown, 1956-57:206).[21]

As Archie Duncan and Al Brown wrote many years ago, 'Unfortunately, the sixty years after 1164 are a dark period in the history of the western seaboard' (ibid:197). Yet we can try to cast a little light on this darkness where Skye is concerned. The island had twelve parish kirks (Munro, 1961:68).[22] This puts me in mind of the six medieval parishes (earlier six districts) of Islay (Lamont, 1966:1-8 and at 72-73), and of the six sheadings of Man (Kinvig, 1975:9-10 and at 12-13); we know that after 1164 the links between Man and Skye were close (Anderson, 1922, ii:458-60). The twelve parishes of Skye may have had an administrative significance, as the Islay districts and Manx sheadings undoubtedly had. It is from the Chronicle of Man that we learn of the existence in Skye, in this very period of darkness, of an administrative officer who might be associated with the twelve parishes. This was Paul, Balki's son, described as 'sheriff' (*vice-comes*) of Skye (ibid:458; Broderick, 1979:f.42v.) — perhaps we should translate this as *syslumaðr*, *sysselman*, 'man of business', factor or in old Scots usage 'doer', administering Skye on behalf of King Olaf. We may discern something of a dynasty here, Balki Paul's father, who would have flourished back in the twelfth century,[23] Paul himself flourishing in the 1220s and 1230s (Anderson, 1922, ii:458-59 and at 478; Broderick, 1979:ff. 42v-43r.) and Paul's son Balki who was active in the Norwegian expedition of 1230-1231 (Anderson, 1922, ii:474-75).

These administrators served the kings of Man, but the dynasty of that island was not a happy band of brothers. Raonall, oldest son of Godfrey II but apparently illegitimate, treated his younger, legitimate, brother Olaf the Black,

---

21 The 'north isles' (Lewis, Harris, Raasay and Skye) were allotted to the kings of Man by the settlement of 1156, while the remaining outer isles, together with the Small Isles, Coll, Tiree, Mull, Jura and Islay went to Somerled and his sons. The inclusion of Harris within Garmoran is probably a mistake.

22 The twelve parishes of Skye might have been traditional lore. Cowan [Cowan, *The parishes of medieval Scotland*, 183] was only able to identify eleven parishes, but he reckoned Kilmalúag in the north of Trotternish to be identical with Kilmuir.

23 Balki father of Paul the sheriff may have been son of a certain noble called Paul who helped King Godfrey the Black against Somerled *c*.1155 [*ESSH*, ii, 231; *CRMI*, f.37v.].

in a very scurvy manner – allotting to him infertile Lewis and, when Olaf complained, having him imprisoned by the king of Scots for over six years (Anderson, 1922, ii:456-57; Broderick, 1979:ff.42v-43r.). Even after Olaf was freed, on King William's death, Raonall and his wife plotted his murder, sending their son Godfrey to Lewis to pursue and kill him (Anderson, 1922, ii:458; Broderick, 1979:f.42v.). By this time Olaf had married a daughter of the new earl of Ross, Ferchar mac an t'sagairt (Anderson, 1922, ii:458; Broderick, 1979:f.42v.). He escaped to the safety of his father-in-law's court and with the help of Paul Balki's son gathered an army with which to attack Godfrey in Skye. They surprised Godfrey and his men sheltering in the little *Eilean Chaluimchille* in Chaluimchille Loch (Loch of Monkstadt) and slew almost all they found (Anderson, 1922, ii:458-59; Broderick, 1979:f.43r.).[24] Against Olaf's wishes, Sheriff Paul had Godfrey blinded and castrated (Anderson, 1922, ii:459).

This is said to have happened in 1223. In 1230 King Hakon IV of Norway decided to sort out all these rebellious and quarrelsome westerners, and also, in the bygoing, put a check to the ambitions of the king of Scots, Alexander II. The Norwegian expedition was not an unqualified success, but from the point of view of the historian of Skye it is noteworthy for introducing us to the forebears of the Macleods, Thorkell son of Thormod and his son, also Thormod (ibid:475).[25] The former was killed in Skye by Sheriff Paul's son Balki (Anderson, 1922:475) — perhaps Thorkell was an adherent of Godfrey son of Reginald. The son, Thormod, was attacked in Lewis by Norwegians returning home — Thormod escaped, but they captured his wife and the great treasure that he possessed (ibid:478). This Macleod treasure on Lewis is interesting in view of the splendid ivory chessmen found at Uig in west Lewis early in the nineteenth century (Glenn, 2003:no.L1 (a)-(c); Stratford, 1997). Perhaps it was only justice (although it sounds very like a thoroughgoing bloodfeud) that Paul

---

24 Eilean Chaluimchille is at NG 377689 (Kilmuir parish). It is in the now drained Loch Chaluimchille. I am grateful to Mr David Sellar for pointing out to me the true site of Godfrey's defeat.

25 The most authoritative and percipient survey of the evidence for MacLeod origins is by Sellar [Sellar, 1997-98, 233-58]. The sources reviewed in that paper do not consider the possibility that the Thorkell and Thormod of Haakon's saga were MacLeod ancestors. The occurrence of Thorkell son of Thormod and his son Thormod in connection with Lewis, Harris and Skye in the 1230s seems too much of a coincidence for them to be of a different lineage from *Sìol Torcuill* (Lewis, Raasay) and *Sìol Thormoid* (Harris, Dunvegan), ancestral to the Macleods.

Balki's son was slain by yet another son of Raonall, Godfrey the Black (Anderson, 1922, ii:478, 544 and at 566).[26]

King Olaf the Black's marriage to Christina of Ross can be seen as the beginning of a Ross interest in Skye, which for all we know, might have been a resumption of interference by the pre-1168 earls. Earl Ferchar was succeeded by his son William (1251-1274) who was closely associated with the Comyn earls of Buchan and their close kinsmen the Comyn lords of Badenoch. The Scottish kingdom was moving inexorably towards the annexation of the Isles. By 1262 Earl William commanded a severely punitive raid on Skye, killing men, women and children and burning or destroying churches and settlements (ibid:605).

Just as Haakon's Saga gives us our earliest chronicle mention of the first Macleods, so it also introduces us to an early, perhaps the earliest, Matheson, Kiarnak Makamal, who collaborated with the earl of Ross in the attack on Skye (ibid:605). This man, as Kermac Macmaghan, figures in the exchequer roll for 1266 (as copied by Sir John Skene in the late sixteenth century) when he seems to have been involved in some royal displeasure incurred by the earl of Ross (Stuart, 1878-1908, i:19-20).[27]

If there is truth in these reports to be found in Haakon's Saga it must mean that the chief men of Skye were believed to have Norwegian sympathies. Yet, as we know, when Haakon came with his big fleet in 1263 he found even the northern isles lukewarm and many in the Sudreys openly loyal to the king of Scots. The Scots were bold enough to have men and ships at Inverie on Loch Nevis (ibid:18-19). In 1264, the year after the battle of Largs but two years before the definitive treaty of Perth, the sheriff of Inverness held only two hostages from Skye (ibid:13) — even if they were the sons of important men it hardly points to deeply felt disaffection. The military operations of the earl of Buchan and Alan Durward were directed mainly at Caithness, but in the summer of 1264 the Scots army was busy subduing the Hebrides, presumably including Skye (ibid:5-6 and at 11; Anderson, 1922, ii:648-49).

No locally produced narrative source comes to our rescue in the later thirteenth century to replace the chatty, informative sagas. The darkness is broken in the early 1290s by the abortive legislation of King John which

---

26 Possibly this was Godfrey *Donn* referred to in this period in the *Chronicle of Man and the Isles*.

27 The form of surname here is closer to the normal Gaelic form than that in Haakon's Saga, but it is clear that the two references are to the same individual.

proposed the establishment of a sheriffdom of Skye, with the earl of Ross as sheriff (Thomson and Innes, 1814-75, i:447b red). Under this plan the importance of Skye itself is emphasized, for the island was to be headquarters of an administrative region stretching from Glenelg, Kintail and Lochcarron in the east to Barra, the Uists and Lewis and Harris in the west. The eight davochs — i.e. ouncelands — of Rum and Eigg were also included (almost certainly with Muck and Canna), and though not explicitly specified we may assume that Raasay and Applecross formed part of the scheme. A very significant phrase in the record of 1293 is 'the king's lands of Skye and Lewis' — this can only refer, surely, to the demesne estates (whichever they were) held in the two islands by the kings of Man and the Isles. And it is precisely this phrase which occurs in a letter written to the king of England in 1297 by Alexander (MacDonald) lord of Islay (Stevenson, 1870, ii:188).[28] The letter is mostly a diatribe against Alexander's distant kinsman Lachlan MacRuairidh, who according to Alexander had with his men been attacking and laying waste the lord king's lands of Skye and Lewis, slaughtering the men, raping the women and burning the king's ships sheltering in church sanctuaries.

There is no doubt that in these years Lachlan was a force to be reckoned with, a bold and ferocious sea-king, with strongholds at Castle Tioram and Kisimul in Barra. In 1299 it was reported to the Scots guardians that Lachlan, in alliance with the earl of Buchan's brother Alexander Comyn, was busy attacking the people of Scotland, burning and laying waste lands and property (Nat.MSS.Scot. 1867-71, ii:no.8; Barrow, 1988:107) Five years later the earl of Atholl feared that the peace of northern Scotland was in serious danger because Lachlan, still allied to Sir Alexander Comyn, had commanded that every ounceland (davoch) — presumably of the Macruairidh lordship of the Isles, but perhaps from further afield including Skye, — was to provide a twenty-oar galley (Bain, 1881-87, ii:no.1633). Even Lachlan appreciated the overwhelming power of King Edward I, to whom he came in person at Ebchester near Durham in August 1306, to swear fealty and ask for the lands of Sir Patrick Graham (Palgrave, 1837:310).

The tumultuous years from 1297 to 1314 are most unlikely to have been peaceful for Skye, but evidence is far to seek. Alexander MacDonald was killed by the MacDougalls in 1299 (McDonald, 1997:168-69), and it does seem that MacDougall adherence to John Balliol pushed the house of Islay into the Bruce

---

28 Note that in this Latin letter the name Lachlan is rendered as Rolandus.

camp. At Bannockburn Bruce was famously supported by Alexander's brother Angus Óg of Islay and since Christina lady of the Isles — senior member of the MacRuairidh family if we confine it to those of legitimate birth — was a relative and close adherent of Bruce (Barrow, 1988:170), while Earl William II of Ross had come into his allegiance in 1309 (ibid:177), we would hardly be indulging in wild speculation to envisage at least a contingent from Skye at the famous battle.

The link between Skye and the earls, if not the earldom, of Ross was strengthened by Robert I, whose sister Matilda was married to Earl William's son and heir Hugh (Cokayne, 1910-59, xi:145; Balfour Paul, 1904-14, vii:236). Before succeeding his father in 1323 Hugh had received from the crown the lands, presumably the crown lands, of Skye and also Trotternish, apparently as a unit distinguishable from Skye as a whole (Thomson, 1882-1914, i:App2. nos.61 and 63). The island itself emerges during the fourteenth century (at latest by 1370) as a *dominium*, lordship (ibid:no.354), but inflation must have set in, for Sleat was a lordship by the 1460s (Munros, 1986:127) and Angus Master of the Isles was styled 'lord of Trotternish' in 1485 (ibid:187) — all the more remarkable since the MacLeods of Dunvegan had charters for Trotternish from John, last MacDonald lord of the Isles (ibid:227-28). Perhaps we come nearer the truth if we note the office of bailie of Trotternish in the fifteenth century (Thomson, 1882-1914, ii:no.2420). A thirteenth-century sheriff or *sysselman* of Skye would have needed bailies. Would it be fanciful to envisage six bailiaries for the island from an early date — Trotternish, Lyndale (or Vaternish), Duirinish, Minginish, Bracadale and Sleat, with two parishes in each — paralleling the six sheadings of Man?

I have said that King John's legislation of 1293 establishing a sheriffdom of Skye was abortive. Of the three new sheriffdoms of that year it has seemed to historians that only Lorn or Argyll became a reality (McNeill and MacQueen, 1996:208-10). But a royal charter of 1541 refers in a completely matter of fact way to 'the sheriffdom of the north isles' (certainly not referring to Orkney and Shetland), (Thomson, 1882-1914, iii:no.2297), including Glenelg and Bracadale. The king toured the isles in the summer of 1540 and was doling out sheriffships for Argyll, Lorn, Knapdale and Kintyre. But fresh appointments to sheriffships are not the same as creating a completely new sheriffdom (Cameron, 1998:246-48).[29]

---

29   The king is said to have inspected the castle of Dunscaich in Sleat (NG 595122).

I have not been able to discover this sheriffdom in record of the fourteenth or fifteenth centuries, nor does it seem to figure anywhere in the Pitlochry Medievalists' *Atlas of Scottish History* (1996). But it cannot be dismissed as a clerical error, still less as fiction. Could it be that since the 1290s, or at least since the reign of Robert I, there was a notional sheriffdom of Skye which simply does not appear in the admittedly scanty record? This sheriffdom would have had some relationship to the bailiaries I have envisaged.

The fleeting glimpse of Earl William III of Ross as lord of Skye in 1370, two years before he died, is almost the last we hear of the island, politically speaking, until Alexander, third MacDonald lord of the Isles, succeeded to the earldom of Ross in 1436. In 1463 Alexander's son and successor John granted 28 merklands of his lordship of Sleat to his half-brother Gilleasbuig (Celestine) for the service of one galley of 18 oars (Munros, 1986:no.80). Six years later the same lands were transferred to John's brother Hugh, already styled 'lord of Sleat', for service expressed in general terms (ibid:no.96). Hugh was ancestor of Donald Gormson, prominent as lord of Sleat in Queen Mary's reign (Dawson, 2002:131, 160, 198 and at 201).

Galley service, general throughout the isles since Norse times, was beginning to fade away, slowly, in the mid-fifteenth century, leaving its traces chiefly in heraldry and on sculptured stones. It raises the question of materials and their availability, for surely the supply of timber big enough and of good enough quality to build a well-found *birlinn* was under threat by the later 1400s? John of the Isles' charter of Sleat for his half-brother Gilleasbuig declares that the land comes with 'wood, oak trees, broom and brushwood', but we must doubt whether this is to be taken literally (Munros, 1986:127).[30] The charter was evidently the work of the lord of the Isles' secretary, Thomas Munro (ibid:liii, 123, 126 and at 154). Most of the surviving documents composed by Munro display such an excess of *formulae* and diplomatic protocol that we are left feeling that he was either determined to give his master his money's worth or else merely showing off (ibid: nos. 78, 79 and 96).[31] Thus oak trees turn up in

---

30 The list of easements and perquisites in the charter, beginning *per omnes rectas metas* and ending *sine revocacione seu reclamacione* reads as though it had been taken from a formulary, including everything for good measure.

31 A series of documents issued by the lord of the Isles between 1461 and 1469 is characterised by the inclusion of elaborate and repetitive *clausulae* of easements and liberties. It may be Munro's stylistic influence that we see in the series as a whole [Munros, *Acts of the Lords of the Isles*, nos. 72, 76, 78, 79, 80, 82, 88, 89 and 96].

charters anent Lochbroom, Lochcarron, Lochalsh, Torridon and Kishorn as well as Creich and Spinningdale in Sutherland (ibid:nos. 76 and 82). I am not suggesting that the oak trees were not there, but of what quality and in what quantity must be unclear. Seven centuries earlier Adamnán abbot of Iona tells us that Columba, staying for a few days on Skye, encountered a wild boar in a dense forest (Sharpe, 1995:175). Alas! I am no palaeobotanist and do not know whether the Western Isles in general or Skye in particular might have been much better provided with significant woodland and sizeable trees in the earlier middle ages than in the days of Johnson and Boswell or in modern times. Martin Martin certainly believed, in 1703, that Skye, as he puts it, 'hath antiently been covered all over with Woods, as appears from the great Trunks of Fir-trees, etc. dug out of the Bogs frequently, etc. There are several Coppices of Wood, scatter'd up and down the Isle; the largest call'd Lettir-hurr, exceeds not three miles in length.' This is Leitir-fura on the coast of Sleat (Martin, 1970:142).[32] Alexander Nicolson, the historian of Skye, says that bog firs are rare in the island but common on Rona (Nicolson, 1994:231).

As is well known, Skye became the seat of those bishops of the Isles who owed allegiance to Scotland, or at least to the *ecclesia Scoticana*, after the English (who had deprived the Scots of the Isle of Man *c.*1333) adhered to the Roman popes in 1387. The Scots remained loyal to the Avignonese popes (Watt and Murray, 2003:257 and at 262-64; Nicolson, 1974:190-93 and at 237-46). In fact it seems that a separate episcopal see had already established itself at Snizort on Skye by the 1320s, though it is only known to have elected one bishop (Watt and Murray, 2003:262). By 1433 the then bishop, Angus, an illegitimate son of Donald lord of the Isles, was petitioning the pope to have his see transferred from Snizort to 'some honest place', probably meaning Iona (Dunlop and MacLauchlan, 1983:25). Thirty years after Angus's death another Angus, almost certainly the first one's son, was provided to the see and duly consecrated at Rome (Watt and Murray, 2003:264). It is perhaps easy to view the distinctly laid back processes by which, first, a bastard son of the lord of the Isles was rapidly ordained priest and then consecrated bishop of the Isles and, second, that bishop's manifestly illegitimate son was appointed to rule the same diocese, as exemplifying an entirely typical West Highland way of doing things. Perhaps they do, but I suspect that in the later fifteenth century there were dioceses very much nearer to Rome where not very dissimilar customs were observed.

---

32 Leitir-fura lies from NG 7115 to NG 7517, and is wooded at the present day.

In any event, we are lucky that the first bishop Angus went to Rome in person in 1428 (Cameron, 1934:8). The record arising from his visit suddenly provides a window through which we can see the name and situation of one Skye clergyman whom the bishop took with him and of others with whom he was connected (Dunlop, 1956:203; Dunlop and Cowan, 1970:19-26).[33] The churches involved were Kilcrist (Cill Chriosd) of Strathsuardal (Strathswordale), Kilchonnan of Uig, and Kilchonnan of Vaternish (Trumpan), all classified as rectories. The clergy, described as subdeacons or in two cases as 'alleged priests', were either (in one case) at Rome, petitioning for favours, or were at home on Skye being petitioned against. The petitioner was Domhnall mac Maelchomghall, subdeacon and parson of the church of St Connán of Uig, annual value 4 merks (Dunlop and Cowan, 1970:26). He was permitted to hold the rectory of Kilcrist in Strathsuardal (value 7 merks) because two clerics in turn had held it for a year without taking priest's orders, namely Donnchadh Mac Dhonnchaidh and Maelcholuim Mac Gillebhrigde. Interestingly, the latter was entitled *rannare*, i.e. a nobleman's household steward or dispenser (Dunlop, 1956:203-04). But not content with these favours, Domhnall was also given leave to take the parish church of St Connan of Vaternish because first Domhnach Mac Gillechoinnich had held it for a year without becoming a priest and then Andrew 'of Buth' (Bute – or perhaps Boath near Nairn?) had detained the church improperly (ibid).

Domhnall seems to have reached Rome in 1428, but evidently did not complete his business there till June 1429 (Dunlop and Cowan, 1970:26). History does not relate whether he survived the summer heat and endemic malaria of Rome to win home to Skye. If he did, his struggles would still not be over unless he could enforce the papal decisions in his favour, possibly with secular help.

We can surely not deny that this record reveals a highly unsatisfactory state of affairs. Parochial livings were bandied about, recklessly it seems, and the Christian faithful were surely in constant doubt as to who their pastor was, or to whom they could turn for the baptism of their children or the burial of their parents. Rapid exchange of benefices was by no means peculiar to Skye or even

---

33 Probably the most authentic form of the petitioner's name appears in [Dunlop and Cowan, *Calendar of Scottish Supplications to Rome, 1428-32*, 25] viz. Donald Macmolcomgayll. His father would have been named as a devotee of St Comgall of Bangor and Tiree. Mr David Sellar thinks it likely that Donald was a Nicolson, of the family ancestral to the Nicolsons of Corrybreac (*per litt.*, 5 Aug., 2003).

to Scotland. In England such benefices were known as 'chop churches', and in his Ford Lectures of 1933 Professor Hamilton Thompson drew attention to the case of the deanery of Chester le Street in County Durham (Hamilton Thomson, 1947:107-08). Vacant by death in 1408, it was given to John Thoralby on 6 April but resigned on 12 April so that John could take the rectory of Lockington in Yorkshire. John Dalton replaced Thoralby at Chester-le-Street but resigned the living on 15 April to Walter Bosum who only a fortnight later exchanged it with Robert Assheburn for the vicarage of St Oswald's, Durham. Thompson writes that during the fourteenth century the custom of exchanging benefices had reached serious proportions and by the end of that century it had developed into an abuse (ibid:107).

What does strike me, however, in the case of Skye is that the ecclesiastical structure was sound and record-keeping adequate. The names, status and values of benefices were preserved and although the scribes or clerks in Rome had severe problems in reproducing west highland personal names they seldom baffle us permanently. I leave you to imagine the clergy and their servants setting out from Skye six hundred and seventy-five years ago on the long, expensive and complicated journey to Rome. Any historian would be thankful that the record generated by their journey has survived.

References

Anderson, A.O. (2 vols. 1922) *Early Sources of Scottish History*. Edinburgh.

Anderson, A.O. and M.O. (rev. ed. 1991) *Adomnan's Life of Columba*. Oxford.

Bain, Joseph (1881-87) *Calendar of Documents relating to Scotland*. Edinburgh.

Balfour Paul, J. (9 vols. 1904-14) *The Scots Peerage*. Edinburgh.

Bannatyne Club (1851-55) *Origines Parochiales Scotiae*. 3 vols., Edinburgh.

Barrow, G.W.S. (3rd edition, 1988) *Robert Bruce and the Community of the Realm of Scotland*. Edinburgh.

Broderick, George (1979) *Cronica Regum Mannie et Insularum*. Man. [*Chron. Man*]

Cameron, A.I. (1934) *The Apostolic Camera and Scottish Benefices, 1418-88*. London.

Cameron, J. (1988) *James V, the personal rule, 1528-1542*. East Linton.

Clancy, T.O. (1995) 'Annat in Scotland and the origins of the parish' *Innes Review*, 46, 91-115.

Cokayne, G.E. (13 vols., 1910-59) *The Complete Peerage*. London.

Cowan, I.B. (1967) *The parishes of medieval Scotland*. Edinburgh.

Crawford, B.E. (1987) *Scandinavian Scotland: Scotland in the early Middle Ages*. Leicester.

Dawson, J. (2002) *The politics of religion in the age of Mary, queen of*

Duncan, A.A.M. and Brown, A.L. (1956-57) 'Argyll and the Isles in the earlier middle ages', *Proceedings of the Society of Antiquaries of Scotland*, 90, 192-220.

Dunlop, A.I. (1956) *Calendar of Scottish Supplications to Rome, 1423-28*. Edinburgh.

Dunlop, A.I. and Cowan, I.B. eds. (1970) *Calendar of Scottish Supplications to Rome, 1428-1432*. Edinburgh.

Dunlop, A.I. and MacLauchlan, D. (1983) *Calendar of Scottish Supplications to Rome, 1433-1447*. Glasgow.

Facsimiles of the National Manuscripts of Scotland (3 vols., 1867-71). London.

Glenn, V. (2003) *Romanesque and Gothic: Decorative Metalwork and Ivory Carvings in the Museum of Scotland*.

Hamilton Thompson, A. (1947) *The English Clergy and their organization in the later middle ages*. Oxford.

Kinvig, R.H. (1975) *The Isle of Man: a social, cultural and political history*. Liverpool.

Lamont, W.D. (1966) *The Early History of Islay*. Dundee.

Mackinlay, J.M. (1914) *Ancient church Dedications in Scotland: non-scriptural dedications*. Edinburgh.

Martin, M. (rep. 1970) *A Description of the Western Islands of Scotland*. Edinburgh.

McDonald, R.A. (1997) *The Kingdom of the Isles*. East Linton.

McNeill, P.G.B. and MacQueen, H.L. (1996) *Atlas of Scottish History to 1707*. Edinburgh.

Munro, R.W. (1961) *Monro's Western Isles of Scotland and Genealogies of the Clans*. Edinburgh.

Munro, J. and Munro R.W. eds. (1986) *Acts of the Lords of the Isles, 1336-1493*. Edinburgh.

Nicolson, A. (rev. ed. 1994) *History of Skye*. Portree.

Nicholson, R. (1974) *Scotland: the later Middle Ages*. Edinburgh.

Old Statistical Account. Edinburgh.

Palgrave, Francis (1837) *Documents and Records Illustrating the History of Scotland*. London.

Richmond, I.A. (1954) *Roman and Native in North Britain*. Edinburgh and London.

Sellar, W.D.H. (1966) 'The origins and ancestry of Somerled' *Scottish Historical Review*, 45, 123-142.

Sellar, W.D.H. (1997-98) 'The Ancestry of the Macleods reconsidered' *Transaction of the Gaelic Society of Inverness*, 60, 233-58.

Sharpe, R. (1995) *Adomnán of Iona: Life of St Columba*. London.

Stevenson, J. (2 vols., 1870) *Documents illustrative of the history of Scotland*. Edinburgh.

Stratford, N. (1997) *The Lewis Chessmen: the enigma of the hoard*. London.

Stuart, J. and others (1878-1908) *The Exchequer Rolls of Scotland*. Edinburgh.

Sutherland, E. (1997) *The Pictish Guide: a guide to the Pictish stones*. Edinburgh.

Thomson, J. M. and others (1882-1914) *Registrum Magni Sigilli Regum Scotorum in Archivis Publicis Asservatum*. London.

Thomson, T. and Innes, C. (1814-75) *The Acts of the Parliaments of Scotland*. Edinburgh.

Watt, D.E.R. and Murray, A.L. (rev. ed. 2003) *Fasti Ecclesiae Scoticanae medii aevi ad annum 1638*. Edinburgh.

Watson, W.J. (1926) The History of the Celtic Place-Names of Scotland. Edinburgh.

"Chaidh a' Chuibhle mun Cuairt"[1] – Skye and the Land Agitation

John Norman MacLeod

THE Highland Land agitation of the 1880s is a theme which has been widely researched and extensively written about, with a particular focus on the years between 1881 and 1886. Skye very much featured in the upheavals of this period and I will look again at the main events, appraise their significance and consider why Skye crofters were to the forefront of agitation at this time? For this talk on the land agitation in Skye, I will confine myself to the same period 1881-86, while recognising that the land agitation, here as elsewhere, extended well beyond this date and even continued after the First World War.

Before looking at events at Braes, Glendale and Kilmuir, it is worth considering some wider aspects of Highland and Islands land agitation. What was the nature and extent of the crofters' resistance? What factors helped to activate and sustain the land agitation of this period? And, indeed, why was there not more of it until the 1880s?

Though the tenantry endured great hardships as a result of the Clearances there is a general viewpoint among historians that tacksmen, crofters and cottars did very little to help themselves before the 1850s, both to resist the removals and extreme provocation they endured at the hands of the landlords.

Despite these claims, there were reported incidents of conflict, even as early as 1792 in Coigach, with around fifty in all reported in the period to 1855. However, up until the 1850s, there was little unified resistance with no sustained attempt by the victims to mount anything approximating to a generalised assault on their oppressors. It can be argued that crofters had decided that resistance was futile and would only end in failure in the face of the apparent ease with which landlords gained backing from central government. Certainly, landlords and the

---

1   *Chaidh a' chuibhle mun cuairt* – The wheel (of fortune) has turned.

authorities dealt with any insurrections with brute force, even when the incident did not merit it.

Though the Irish and Scottish Highlanders were part of a single Gaelic-speaking civilisation that also shared hunger, famine, clearance and emigration into the nineteenth century, the Highlanders certainly refused to engage in death dealing protest as their Irish counterparts did. Though, as Hunter points out, they were well equipped to do so through their martial traditions and military experience of serving in the British armed forces (Hunter, 1999:Chap.8). In relation to the land questions there were significant differences in circumstances that may have contributed to the Scottish Highland disinclination to rebel. Irish landowners, of British extraction, were generally English in speech and Protestant in religion and, as such, were regarded as alien intruders. In contrast, the Highlanders still clung to the concept of *dùthchas*,[2] regarding their landlords as the descendents of their hereditary clan chiefs and the people could not readily break with traditional loyalties.

When exploring the nature and scale of Highland resistance, it is important to note that there was probably more resistance than reported and also that, as much of the resistance was unsuccessful, it was ultimately forgotten. It is also important to recognise that there is more than one type of resistance. In addition to physical resistance there is more passive and indirect forms of protest — as successfully undertaken in the rent strikes in Skye during the 1880s and in the early American civil rights movement of the 1960s.

During the latter half of the nineteenth century the people of the Scottish Highlands and Islands were demoralised in many ways, their language, culture and traditions were routinely denigrated and they were ridiculed by external observers as being in abject apathy. As Prebble has noted: "People accepted the introduction of sheep in the same manner that they accepted famine and pestilince" (Prebble, 1963). With few political solutions at this time to their problems, they tended to look back rather than forward. In many ways they were not alone as the poorer classes in Britain were equally politically disadvantaged.

What was particularly evident in the pre-1850 period was the lack of leadership, with a number of the tacksman class having already emigrated. Like others who have also been in a similar situation, the Highlanders sought collective relief from their sufferings in the sphere of religious experience. The Disruption of the Church in 1843 and the associated emergence of the Free

---

2   *dùthchas* – traditional clan lands, with authority recognised from within the clan itself.

Church, provided "emotional and ideological cohesion" (MacPherson Robertson, 1995:75). The role of the nineteenth century evangelism, in the form of hugely charismatic lay preachers, who were normally from a Gaelic crofting background, helped to counter the psychological dislocation produced by the collapse of clanship. They also provided leadership that compensated, to some extent, for the loss of the tacksmen, with the overall impact central to the emergence of a crofter consciousness from the 1850s onwards. In some cases, where there were disturbances, the role of the local minister was as a mediator, as in the parish of Kilmuir in 1884.

Despite this, and according to Richards, the resistance up until the mid-nineteenth century had checked the full exercise of landlord power and had attracted public support that proved effective in the 1880s. He linked events to "a century-long tradition of sporadic popular resistance" (Richards, 1973:36). Withers also saw continuity in the agitation, with crofters possessing a legitimising ideology of the expressed belief in the customary occupation of land. In the period 1850 to 1880, Grigor and others identified a new stage in the landlord-centred conflict in the Highlands and Islands, with demands now for the restoration of the land, end to evictions and to arbitrarily imposed rent increases (Grigor, 2000: Chap.4).

So what had changed by the 1880s? Certainly, forms of communication had greatly improved with the development of a steamer service and the extension of the railways into the North and West Highlands to railheads like Stromeferry (Wester Ross), served to facilitate travel and seasonal migration to the south for employment. The later introduction of the telegraph allowed news to travel more readily and the Skye crofters used this new means of communication to keep abreast of the movements of the Government authorities.

In the 1880s there was also a developing interest in Gaelic culture, both at a popular and an academic level. Second generation Highlanders in urban Scotland were among the most enthusiastic supporters of crofting agitation in the 1880s and they formed Clubs and Societies in the larger population centres. For example, the formation of the Gaelic Society of Inverness in 1871, encouraged the setting up of other similar groups in Glasgow and Greenock. The same enthusiasts also successfully campaigned for the foundation of a chair of Celtic at the University of Edinburgh and it was the same Gaelic Inverness enthusiasts who first petitioned parliament for a royal commission into the Highland land question.

Poets like Mary MacPherson (Màiri Mhòr, the Skye Poetess), played an important role in encouraging the people to take action in creating a new social and political order. In the columns of *The Highlander*, John Murdoch reported on events in Ireland and demonstrated a clear vision for the Highlands and Islands, suggesting that as the Highlanders and the Irish had a common Gaelic culture, that they work together to achieve the overthrow of landlords. Along with Alexander MacKenzie's Celtic Magazine, later termed *The Scottish Highlander*, Murdoch relentlessly petitioned for more Gaelic in schools. Even after the demise of *The Highlander* in 1881, he remained as a strong figure in the land reform movement.

In the 1870s and 1880s there was a changing attitude among the people, with a new generation emerging more versed in the politics of the day. Growing crofter self-consciousness also emerged from the post-1846 evictions, which was compounded by the improved economic conditions of the 1860s and 1870s. The younger generation, though they did not directly experience the evictions, were well versed in the history of their fore-bearers and, in any case, the record of dispossession was still clearly evident on the surface of the land. Though crofters' conditions had improved by the 1880s, it must be remembered that there was still widespread distress and suffering, with threat of famine always looming.

Of course Skye was not the only area where insurrection took place at this time. However conditions and feelings of injustice were particularly high on the island, further intensified by the crop failures and severe famine conditions resulting from the violent storms of 1882-83. The wages of west coast fishermen had deteriorated and Skye fishermen and crofters, who had witness of what was happening in Ireland, were more inclined to resist their landlords than at any time before. Newspapers, expecting confrontation, thrust events in Skye into the national limelight and, as the island had also been chosen by the authorities as the place to stamp out any crofter insurrection and to make an example of any agitators, the ingredients for insurrection were right.

The Skye Land Wars

The authorities and newspaper reporters did not have to wait long for confrontation. The first example of direct action by the Skye crofters in the war against landlordism commenced at Valtos in 1881 on the Kilmuir estate. Here, the crofters gave notice that they would no longer pay extortionately high rents on the estates of Major William Fraser, the most hated landlord in Skye at this time. The rent strike had followed an unsuccessful petition asking for a rent reduction. John Murdoch was quick to condemn Major Fraser and, as a sign of the growing interest and publicity for the cause, the Irish Nationalist and Land League Leader Charles Stewart Parnell addressed a mass meeting in Glasgow, condemning landlords like Fraser for their actions. As Alexander MacDonald, Lord MacDonald's factor later reported, "that was the beginning of it". In the same year, the crofters of Glendale followed the Kilmuir crofter's example, combining rent-strike tactics with direct land occupation.

It was in Braes, however, in 1881 and 1882 that the first serious blow was struck for the people of the Highlands and Islands and it was the aftermath of these incidents that attracted nation-wide interest in the crofters' struggle.

1882 – The Battle of the Braes

As early as 1865, the Braes crofters had been deprived of their grazing rights on Ben Lee when they were added to a large sheep farm. In addition, the crofting townships of Gedintaylor, Balmeanach and Peinchorran had become seriously overcrowded as a result of evictions from Sconser and Loch Sligachan. Passions among the crofters were beginning to run high and the issue came to a head in 1881, when the Braes men had returned from fishing in Kinsale, in the south-west of Ireland. While there, they had learnt of the land struggle and, encouraged by the success of the Irish Land League Movement, they presented a carefully worded petition to Lord MacDonald asking that their former pastures in Skye be restored to them. Later, at Martinmas, they marched to Portree and informed the factor, Alexander MacDonald, "that no rents would be paid until Ben Lee was returned to them."

Lord MacDonald responded by ordering that a dozen Braes crofters be evicted. On 7 April 1882 a sheriff-officer was despatched from Portree to serve the eviction notices. The Braes people were ready and he was intercepted, papers were wrenched from his grasp and burnt. The crime of deforcement had now been committed and the authorities were thus enabled to move against them with all the force that could be mustered for that task.

William Ivory, the sheriff of Inverness-shire, decided to act quickly and to take personal charge of an expeditionary force that he now planned to send against the Braes crofters. As there were insufficient officers in Inverness, reinforcements were sought from other forces with a detachment of forty to fifty constables from Glasgow answering the urgent call. At dawn on 19 April they marched on Braes led by Ivory himself. The Braes people were taken by surprise and the five ringleaders were arrested with a view to them being imprisoned in Portree. By now the Braes people had been mobilised and the officers faced a hostile mob as they negotiated their return journey through the small crofting township of Gedintaylor. A fierce struggle followed, with stones and rocks being hurled at the authorities. A determined baton charge allowed the police detachment to break through the mob and, in a state of some disorder, they retreated to the comparative safety of Portree.

When sheriff officers attempting to serve summonses on the Braes crofters were again deforced on 2 September and on 24 October 1882, despite being accompanied on the second occasion by eleven policemen, Sheriff Ivory of Inverness felt strongly that the law in Skye must be "vindicated". He asked the Government for gunboats and marines. Sir William Harcourt, Home Secretary in the Liberal Government from 1880 to 1885, was reluctant to comply with the request, claiming such action could only be justified if the ordinary processes of the law had broken down and civil disorder was present or imminent.

The Braes dispute was settled at the end of 1882, with the crofters' fines having been paid by supporters. Lord MacDonald agreed to a compromise and the people once again turned their stock on to Ben Lee. Braes had become a catalyst for much wider resistance and the skirmish was the prelude to more widespread acts of sustained subordination in Skye, Glendale, Kilmuir, and also further afield.

The Glendale Martyrs

John MacPherson, Milovaig, was the recognised leader of the Glendale crofters who organised defiance of the Court of Session interdict forbidding grazing of cattle on Waterstein farm in 1881. When the crofters drove their livestock on to the former grazings they were subsequently removed by the local shepherds, who themselves then encountered physical abuse from the crofters. As the resistance escalated, Ivory again clamoured for military action. However, the police sent to serve notices on the ring-leaders were driven from the glen and even when further police reinforcements arrived in Loch Dunvegan, on the mailboat *Dunara Castle*, they decided that it was best not to engage the huge mob of youths confronting them.

Early in 1882, as a show of force, the gunboat *Jackal* anchored in Loch Pooltiel. Malcolm MacNeill, later to be Secretary of the Royal Commission, persuaded the Glendale leaders to recognise the rule of law and go of their own will to court in Edinburgh. They duly left on the *Dunara Castle*, an action viewed as a "victory for tact and common sense". Four Glendale men, including John MacPherson, were to serve a two-month prison sentence in Calton Jail, Edinburgh. While there they were visited by leading politicians, including Joseph Chamberlain. On 15 May 1882, the 'Glendale Martyrs' were released and when they disembarked from the steamer at Portree a large crowd congregated and John MacPherson was carried aloft for a joyous celebration at the Portree Hotel.

Thereafter, MacPherson was to become a major figure in the Highland Land Law Reform Association (HLLRA) or as it later became popularly known, The Highland Land League. At the first public meeting of the League in Glendale he argued that "the land should belong to the people who work it." He was a natural leader and orator and was to become the crofters' spokesman, not only in Glendale but also throughout Scotland. It was the continuing agitation of the Glendale crofters that influenced the Government in establishing, in March 1883, the Royal Commission of Inquiry into the Conditions of the Highlands and Islands of Scotland (The Napier Commission).

The establishing of the Napier Commission slowed the agitation. However, there was continuing disquiet among the crofters that matters were taking too long and in October 1884 the insurrection resumed. Firstly, 1000 crofters gathered at Quirang in Staffin and a resolution was unanimously passed against Major Fraser of Kilmuir and which also disowned Alexander MacDonald as factor.

Thereafter, on 31 October 1884 a group of nine police officers set forth from Portree en-route to Uig but they were blocked by a jeering crowd of 200 crofters and forced back to Portree. This incident induced Ivory to make yet another plea to A.J. Balfour, the Lord Advocate, for a gunboat and marines. In the light of sensational newspaper reports of impending trouble, the Government, following a seven-hour debate, reluctantly agreed. William Harcourt, the Home Secretary had confessed more anxiety over the Skye crofters and their plight than over the Irish 'Dynamitards'. Harcourt was sympathetic to the crofters and he once again condemned the proprietors for their greed. He was of the opinion that some of the Skye landlords had brought about the troubles now facing them and he cited the increase in the Kilmuir rents from £3,000 to £7,000 as one of the immediate causes and appealed to them to make sacrifices to solve the questions (MacPhail, 1976:64 and at 75). The military expedition arrived first in Portree on Sunday, 16 November. The forces included HMS *Assistance*, a troopship, two gunboats the *Forester* and the *Banterer*. Macbrayne's steamer, the *Lochiel*, was commissioned as a mobile police barracks when it became apparent that none of the island's innkeepers were willing to identify themselves with the forces of law and order by providing accommodation for policemen.

On 18 November, the military force of over 400 marines and fifty extra police armed with revolvers landed at Uig. Though Sheriff Ivory claimed that the Kilmuir crofters committed a deforcement, the Lord Advocate decided not to prosecute, as he decided that the people had opposed the police only because they were regarded as agents of the landlords.[3]

John MacPherson counselled the people not to resist and, following pacific pleas from members of the Land League, MacPherson and Duncan Cameron, a reporter from the Oban Times, went aboard the *Lochiel* and assured the Government forces that there would be no trouble. Sheriff Ivory refused to call off the expedition. The sixteen newspaper reporters from the south that had gathered there in expectation of a confrontation were to be disappointed.

In the face of such military force, the people engaged in acts of passive resistance. The telegraph system was used to good effect to warn crofters of the movement of Ivory's forces and in areas like Glendale and Kilmuir a horn or *dùdach mòr* was sounded to warn the crofters of their imminent arrival. Six hundred people were in attendance at one meeting in Glendale and when marines arrived the leaders immediately launched into prayers. Meanwhile, in Kilmuir, the rent strikes continued.

Marches to Kilmuir and Glendale had little effect to dampen the spirits of the crofters and it was soon evident that there was little for the marines to do. Already, the *Lochiel* and the extra police had been withdrawn, causing a quarrel between Harcourt and Ivory. Harcourt saw this as saving expenses for the County, while the exchequer continued to fund the marines. The marines received farewell messages from the local people and in Staffin, they seem to have shown an even greater interest in the women, with a crofter, William Nicolson remarking "they gave more of their time to the god of love than to the god of war".

---

3   The Inverness County Police Committee was composed almost entirely of landlords at this time.

Major Fraser at this time urged Alexander MacDonald to serve summonses on those who were in rent-arrears, given that the marines were on the island but A.J. Balfour made it clear that troops had not been deployed for such purposes. As a concession, Fraser himself decided to offer a 25% reduction in the rent, which only served to reinforce the crofters' conviction that their rents had previously been much too high. If anything, the resolutions of the crofters seemed to have strengthened since the arrival of the military expedition.

When a sheriff-officer from Portree was deforced on his way to Kilmuir in December, 1884 three crofters were arrested and tried. One of the accused, Norman Stewart "Parnell" of Valtos and the leader of the Kilmuir crofters, successfully defended himself. Prior to the trial, Ivory had issued a libellous statement against Stewart and he now had to suffer the humiliation of losing the case and having to pay £25 damages. Other deforcements occurred in Glendale, Waternish and Kilmuir against an officer from Inverness who had been brought in as a replacement, as local sheriff officers refused to serve summonses. The deforcers in Glendale were only given mild sentences by the Sheriff-substitute, Spiers, who showed sympathy for the grievances leading to the agitation. In addition to a sheriff officer, the legal system required a concurrent also but local ground officers were reluctant to become involved. The legal system in Skye was now under great strain, much to the frustration of Alexander MacDonald. He concluded that the acquittal of Stewart and the mild sentences handed to the Glendale deforcers only encouraged further lawlessness. The marines eventually left Skye in June 1885 when the men-folk departed for the herring fishing.

Despite efforts from the landlords, many of them by now on a rate strike and forming their own association in an attempt to hang on to an untenable position, a Crofters Bill was finally presented to the House of Commons. When it became the Crofters' Act in 1886, it gave security of tenure and introduced a system of judicially-determined rents. The evictions if not the agitation had been brought to an end.

The Act, though an important landmark in crofting history, did not restore to crofters land lost as a result of earlier evictions. Unrest consequently continued in the form of land seizures. Troops were again sent to Skye in 1886 and to Sutherland and Lewis in the following two years.

Though the confrontations between the crofters and the authorities took place in the townships of Braes, Glendale and Kilmuir; Portree was to act as the nerve centre of the campaign. It was here information was gathered and sent out to the crofters. It is interesting to note that the village was split on the agitation issue, with a small establishment party convinced that life and property was at risk from Fenian revolutionaries who had flamed the crofters. The establishment based itself at the Royal Hotel, while the crofter's friends used the Portree Hotel. A couple of incidents give a flavour to the local mood at the time.

On Monday, 4 October 1886, the whisper went round that the hated Sheriff Ivory was on his way with another military expedition. By 7pm, as the steamer *Glencoe* drew in to Portree pier, a crowd of approximately 300 people had gathered. As Ivory stepped ashore, accompanied by numerous plain clothes police, he was greeted with "a perfect tempest of booing and groaning" and according to the Scottish Highlander's reporter the crowd followed him to the Royal Hotel with "howls of derision".

By contrast, when Michael Davitt, the founder of the Irish Land League, toured the Highlands and Islands in 1887, he was greeted with wild excitement when he embarked at Portree on Saturday 7 May. It is estimated that thousands packed Somerled Square to hear him speak from the window of his room in the Portree Hotel. Skye's staunchly Protestant crofters even invited Davitt, himself a Catholic, to be their Parliamentary candidate. It was very apparent throughout his journey that the Gaels supported the Irish in their campaign for more political freedom and, similarly, he demonstrated that he was most familiar with issues and problems in the Highlands and that he greatly sympathised with them. At Stromeferry he remarked:

> [...] I have felt more strongly than ever the link of sympathy which binds me to the Celtic race of the Highlands. The exterminator's hand which has depopulated Ireland has also been busy with destruction here.

He advised the Highlanders that they should not satisfy themselves with security of tenure but that they should recover, from the landowners, the land they lost at the time of the Clearances. He went as far as to suggest that landlords, sporting estates and deer should all be got rid of.

> The day of the people is at hand when the rule of the classes shall give way to that of the masses, when landlordism must go the way of every other tyranny that has been struck down by the people's might, and when the system of extermination and legalised robbery, which has ruined Ireland and depopulated the Highlands, shall be banished for ever from our midst.

As a consequence of all this activity it can be argued that the Skye land agitation of this period was very significant. It was in Skye that the first meetings of the Highland Land League and the Napier Commission were held. Crofters like John MacPherson, Norman Stewart and the Rev Donald MacCallum (the Church of Scotland minister of Waternish), were to become notable champions of the crofters movement in the Highlands and Islands. Undoubtedly their example and the events of 1881-86 encouraged other crofters within the area to take the initiative to regain their grazing rights and to try and win back their lands. The historic events at Braes attracted nation-wide interest, with questions being raised in the House of Commons, and they were to have far-reaching effects in respect of the Highlands and Islands regaining some part of the autonomy it had lost during the eighteenth and nineteenth centuries. It is interesting to note that Skye featured as highly in Governmental thoughts at this time as events related to Ireland like the infamous Phoenix Park murders. Harcourt, though, had a great regard for the people of Skye, having sailed to the West Highlands and Islands for a number of years.

The crofters had to wait until 1897, with the setting up of a Congested Districts Board, for an agency with purchase powers, enabling redistribution of former sheep farms. In 1904, both the Glendale and Kilmuir estates passed into public ownership. It was only in Glendale that ownership of the land was transferred to the crofters themselves. The crofters in Kilmuir still pay rent to the Secretary of State or more correctly, the Scottish Executive Rural Affairs Department (SERAD). Later Crofting Acts created new crofts and transferred the land to the people. Recent years have seen, the formation of a Crofters Union and even more radical political initiatives in relation to crofting and community ownership. The spirit and radical tradition of John MacPherson and Mairi Mòr lives on and for those communities in Skye and elsewhere who now have control over their own land and resources: *Tha a' Chuibhle air tionndadh – tha an roth air a dhol mun cuairt* (The wheel has certainly turned full-circle).

References

Grigor, I.F. (2000) *Highland Resistance*. Edinburgh.

Hunter, J. (1999) *Last of the Free*. Edinburgh.

MacPhail, I.I.M. (1976) *The Skye Military Expedition of 1884–85*, TGSI, 48, 62-94.

MacPhail, I.I.M. (1989) *The Crofters' War*. Stornoway.

MacPherson Robertson, I.J. (1995) *The Historical Geography of Social Protest in Highland Scotland*, 1914 – *c*.1939. Unpublished PhD Thesis, University of Bristol.

Prebble, J. (1963) *The Highland Clearances*. London.

Richards, E. (1973) *How tame were the Highlanders during the Clearances?*, Scottish Studies, No. 17, 35-50.

Some Reflections on the Poetry of Skye

Aonghas MacNeacail

APART from a couple of not altogether successful attempts at writing novels in the early twentieth century by Angus Robertson and the Rev. Neil Ross, and the writings, in both fiction and non-fiction of the Rev Kenneth MacLeod, Skye has not really been explored in prose by Gaelic writers. Exceptions are the fictions of Eilidh Watt and Maoilios Caimbeul (the latter more readily identified as a poet), and the journalism of Martin MacDonald. The one native Skye prose writer of international repute, Martin Martin, left nothing, as far as we know, in the language which must surely have been his first.

Alternatively, writers like Seton Gordon, who settled on the island, Derek Cooper, who was of Skye descent, Alan Campbell MacLean, and Margaret MacPherson, and poets like Richard Hugo and Hugh MacDairmid, have all contributed to placing the island firmly on the literary map, but in English.

To get a Gaelic literary perspective on Skye, therefore, we have to look to the poets. Of these there is no shortage and this is true of the world of Gaelic generally. While there is an ancient tradition of storytelling, the stories, being of anonymous authorship, often taking on local details and characteristics, may be said to belong to the entire community, and will frequently have international provenance. The poetry is where we are most likely to find the individual creative voice articulating a specific perception of its environment — actual, historical or imagined.

In Skye, as elsewhere in Gaeldom, poetry may be seen to divide into two basic strands. From early times, there has been a formal domain of professionally trained bards who spoke for their designated clans. Even when the bardic caste had been dissolved, a number of formally untrained poets chose to perpetuate the panegyric tradition. Among these was Mairi Nighean Alasdair Ruaidh, one of several seventeenth and eighteenth century Gaelic poets who adopted, or were adopted into, the role of clan bard. Domhnall nan Oran, father of Niall MacLeoid and Iain Dubh Dhomhnaill nan Oran, maintained the custom into the nineteenth century, but was one of the last to do so.

The other poetic order to which Skye has made a distinguished contribution is that which may be called the song tradition. Examples can be found that are clearly of considerable pedigree, and which continued to thrive into the late twentieth century. They still thrive, if we include the works of Uist-born but partly Skye-raised brothers, Calum and Rory MacDonald, the Runrig songsters.

Skye had its representatives of the old Bardic caste. The O' Muirigheasains have been identified in the service of the MacLeods in the seventeenth and eighteenth centuries, while Cathal MacMhuirich, a member of the noted Clanranald bardic family, appears to have transferred his allegiance from Clan Ranald to MacDonald of Sleat sometime in the mid seventeenth century. Cathal's poems include an elegy to John MacLeod of Dunvegan and one commemorating the daughter of Donald Gorm of Sleat. There were, no doubt, many more in a tradition shared by Scotland and Ireland, and with recorded examples traceable back to the thirteenth century. Clan Neacail and MacKinnon, among others, may have been of lesser power and influence than the 'big two', but their chiefs presumably aspired to employ the most essential retainers associated with their status. Whether such lesser figures could provide full-time employment for a bard is debatable, but there is also evidence of a caste of itinerant bards, whose services could presumable by hired for fixed or flexible periods of time.

In Skye, as elsewhere, the profession of Clan bard came under pressure from central authority. In 1609 the Statutes of Iona committed chiefs to "the banishment of vagrant bards" which would lead to the eventual dissolution of the professional caste of trained bards. This did not, however, cause an immediate separation between the clan aristocracies and the practice of poetry.

In an essentially oral culture, it was not unusual for tradition-bearers, including poets, to retain tens of thousands of lines of poetry, from which they could recite squibs or epics at the drop of a hat. Aspiring bards did not have to go far to gain access to the works of past masters. Not having completed years of study like professional poets, these youngsters were unlikely to be skilled in the classical language of their predecessors. However, having heard the material, or versions of it, they would have known its shape and content, and been able to articulate those conventions through their own vernacular.

And once they had begun to master the craft themselves, those bards by inclination could still rely on a cultural continuity that ensured a welcome for their panegyrics from a Gaelic aristocracy (as well as a relatively homogenous community) still aware of their heritage.

One of the most notable of those "unofficial clan bards" who came to prominence in the seventeenth century, was a member of that aristocracy. She was Mary MacLeod, known to the Gaelic world as Mairi Nighean Alasdair Ruaidh. Although born in Harris, not Skye, she was closely associated with the MacLeods of Dunvegan, and spent a considerable part of her life on the island.

John Macinnes referred to her as "one of the most important mediators between classical and vernacular Gaelic", whose "essentially formal court poetry, almost wholly confined to the affairs and personages of Clan MacLeod" was "distinguished by its rhetorical assurance, the clarity of its imagery and its declamatory eloquence."

Although the clan society she lived in may have seemed outwardly stable it was, in reality, a society in transition. First, one of the key elements in the Statutes of Iona had committed Highland chiefs to providing their heirs with a southern education, thus introducing succeeding generations of the Gaelic aristocracy to the metropolitan fleshpots. Second, the so-called "Union of the Crowns" had shifted the seat of political power Edinburgh to London. Together, these developments began the process of alienating the clan aristocracy from their own communities and the culture that defined them.

Mairi Nighean Alasdair Ruaidh's subtle observations about the effects of those trends on the equilibrium of her society earned her the displeasure of her sponsors. In fact, she was exiled from Dunvegan on at least one occasion — though for the most part, her poetry resounds with praise of her kinsmen, their qualities and attributes. A number of her poems have retained their popularity in the Gaelic song tradition, "*An Talla bu Ghnath le MacLeoid*" (The Hall where MacLeod was at ease) being one of the best known. Said to have been written as a premature elegy for Sir Norman MacLeod, who was apparently still alive at the time of its composition, it carries a strong sense of a broader change of circumstance than would have been effected by the passing of a single individual.

Iain MacCodrum was a contemporary of Alasdair Mac Mhaighstir Alasdair, and would have been barely into his teens when Mairi Nighean Alasdair Ruaidh died in the first decade of the eighteenth century. Iain also became a clan bard and was still attached to MacDonald of Sleat in his seventieth year in a similar arrangement as Mairi Nighean Alasdair Ruaidh had with MacLeod of Dunvegan. Iain seems to have spent most of his life in his native North Uist, from which he wryly observed the activities of his neighbours as well as demonstrating a remarkable awareness of the activities of the wider world, national and international. A noted seanchaidh, he was said to be able to recite the poems of Ossian for hours on end.

A dialogue between a friend and enemy of whisky, as well as a song in dispraise of Domhnall Ban's bagpipes are characteristic examples of his poetry, which also includes a number of praise poems and elegies to MacDonald dignitaries. While we cannot truly claim Iain as a domiciled Skye bard in the same sense as Mairi Nighean Alasdair Ruaidh, he no doubt visited Sleat on more than one occasion since he was bard to Clan Donald.

An Ciaran Mabach, otherwise Archibald MacDonald, was an illegitimate son of Sir Alexander MacDonald, 16th Baron of Sleat and chief of Clan Donald. There are only a very few surviving poems by this seventeenth century contemporary of Iain Lom, the Lochaber poet. A couple are elegies to his brother Sir James, but the work that lends him distinction is a poem known by its second line, "*B' Annsa Cadal air Fraoch*". This piece of work demonstrates that the poet was a precursor to Duncan Ban MacIntyre as a celebrant of nature, and in particular of the deer.

The imaginative intensity may not be sustained for as long as it is in MacIntyre's great pibroch poem, "*Moladh Beinn Dorain*", yet MacDonald's treatment of his subject is both novel and effective. He addresses the deer, individually and collectively, as his beloved (neatly punning on the similarity between the words "*graidh*" for herd and "*gradh*" for love), while at the same time perceiving stag and hind as lovers making their evening tryst.

Another noted Skye poet of the seventeenth century (and who lived into the eighteenth) was a native of Strath, and a member of the MacKinnon gentry, Lachlann Mac Thearlaich Oig. Like *An Ciaran Mabach* Lachlann had a distinctive relationship with "the blanket" though his was as producer of, rather than produced, illegitimate children. He is best known for his indictment of the aristocracy of his native island. On one occasion, while he was down on his luck, he was refused hospitality at Dunvegan and composed a poem about the experience. In this poem, variously known as "*Latha Siubhal Sleibh*" (One Day, Travelling the Moor) and "*Oran do Dhaoine Uaisle Araidh*" (A Song to Certain Gentry), he imagines meeting the three qualities of Generosity, Love and Liberality who were outcasts like himself from the great houses of the Highlands.

In a note on the poem in his anthology of eighteenth century verse, Ronald Black referred to such a personification of abstractions as non-Gaelic. He suggested its derivation came from contemporary English Augustan verse since MacKinnon spent three years at school in Nairn, where he is said to have learned to write both poetry and prose in English. Like Mairi Nighean Alasdair Ruaidh, Lachlann was an unwitting observer of, and commentator on, social and political shifts which were gnawing at the underbelly of the old Gaelic world and which would eventually destroy that world forever.

There were also better times for Lachlann. He is recorded as having been a member of an informal literary group known as the 'Talisker Circle', who met at the home of John MacLeod of Talisker. Other members included Roderick Morrison, known as *An Clarsair Dall* (The Blind Harper), *Am Piobaire Dall* (The Blind Piper), otherwise known as John MacKay, and *Iain Mac Ailein* (John MacLean).

Of all the members of this group only MacLean, from Mull and descended from an Ardgour chief, was recorded as bearing the title "Aos-Dana", giving him status as a senior poet, if not formally the clan bard. Other than being an occasional visitor, his connections to Skye seem unclear. Both his fellow visitors had more obvious links. Morrison, a poet as well as harpist, was born in Bragar, Isle of Lewis, received his musical training in Ireland, and became Dunvegan's unofficial clarsair in 1681. Seven years later, political differences caused him to remove from Dunvegan, but he seems to have returned to Dunvegan later in life and was buried there. MacKay, also a poet, blind only from the age of seven, learned his piping skills from Padraig Og Mac Cruimein, of the legendary Boreraig family.

For the purposes of our theme, though, MacKay's most significant Skye connection derives from his daughter's marriage to a man from Strath, which gave him a grandson called Uilleam Ros. Every culture has its troughs and peaks; periods when there is a sense of marking time. During such periods verse and prose is often craftmanlike, pleasing to the audience, but with no sense of edge, of taking risks, of making something new. Then, there comes a time when the energy starts to flow, where there is a new focus and things begin to happen. The eighteenth century was one such period for Gaelic poetry, to which Uilleam Ros was central.

While Neil Mac Mhuirich, who may be counted the last of the great Mac Mhuirich bardic family, was still writing poetry in the classical language (as well as the vernacular) during the eighteenth century, this period is perhaps best characterised by its "new wave" of poets. While these poets were deeply aware of the bardic tradition, they also brought something else to the craft. Alexander MacDonald (Alasdair Mac Mhaighstir Alasdair) son of a Moidart clergyman, was the unquestioned driving force in this tide of innovation. He was first poet to marry the framework of ceol mor, or piobaireachd, as it's more generally known, to the making of poetry. He composed poems on the seasons and he wrote the epic account of a galley's voyage, "*Birlinn Chlann Raghnaill.*" which remains one of the greatest single achievements in Gaelic literature. With praise poems for whisky, plaid and language, and lament for a pet pigeon, he could be said to have brought vernacular material as well as language into the mainstream of Gaelic verse.

As Hugh MacDiarmid provided a lodestone for lowland Scottish poets in the twentieth century, and Sorley MacLean did likewise for the Gael, Mac Mhaighstir Alasdair was the model for his younger contemporaries. Duncan Ban MacIntyre used the piobaireachd form to praise a mountain in his "*Moladh Beinn Dorain*". Like the literate Mac Mhaighstir Alasdair, Rob Donn, who could neither read nor write, used the access he was given to the English satirical poetry of Alexander Pope (read to him by the local minister) to give a new resonance to his poetry. There were others, like the aforementioned MacCodrum and Sileas na Ceapaich, whose work included hymns, praise poems and laments, including the noted song "*Alasdair a Gleanna Garadh.*"

Finally, there was also Uilleam Ros. Educated in Forres, he spent most of his short life in his mother's native Gairloch, where he worked as a schoolmaster, although he first had the opportunity to travel throughout the Highland and Islands with his father who had obtained work as a peddler. Those travels were to provide Ros with the encounter that would provide him with the central theme of his work, the object of the poems on which his reputation essentially stands. When he was in Stornoway he met and fell in love with his kinswoman, Marion Ross.

But he was equally eloquent on other themes. I would doubt whether any Gael, of a certain age, who studied Gaelic at school, does not recognise the words that form the opening couplet to his "*Oran an t-Samhraidh*" (Song of Summer).

> *O mosglamaid gu suilbhir ait,*
> *le sunndachd ghasd, is eireamaid* [...]
> (O let's awake with merry joy,
> with ardent speed, and get up [...])

The language is heightened, dense and rich, the poetic craft intricate: the whole effect is to convey a tremendous sense of exhilaration.

Another of his songs, this time in praise of Gairloch, is presented in the form of a sequence of reflections during a journey through the Southern Highlands where, as an asthmatic and consumptive, he had been sent for the sake of his health. In contrast, a poem in praise of whisky reveals the lighter side of Uilleam Ros. His refrain for the poem quotes Mairi Nighean Alasdair Ruaidh, *"Ho ro, gur toigh leinn drama"* (Ho ro, we like our dram), while the verses variously offer the drink as a cure for stammering, send an old man to flirting, and make the miser a warm host, among other attributes. He also had his own "Holy Willie" to deal with, a moralistic schoolmaster who blotted his copybook by impregnating his own maidservant.

His lament for Charles Edward Stuart — *"Soraidh Bhuan do'n t-Suaineas Bhan"* (Last Farewell to the White Cockade) — reads as the personal statement of a Jacobite sympathiser, not the conventional *"cumha"* we might have expected from one who deferred to tradition, adopted traditional modes. Like his contemporaries, Ros was immersed in those traditions, but he was also a man of his times.

But if those poems are coloured by aspects of his personality, social or political, the love poetry, which, for succeeding generations, has defined him, is infused with a sense of the man's deepest being. Rejected by Marion Ross and further stricken by news of her marriage to a Mersey sea-captain, the joy he expressed on first meeting her turned to the most melodic despair.

Some of his poems also demonstrate his literary sophistication. In *"Cuachag nan Craobh"*, he addresses his complaint to a cuckoo that strikes up its call in a tree beneath which he happens to be lying. His song *"Oran Cumhaidh"* (Song of Lament) incorporates the traditional tale of an Irish harper who threatened murder in the name of love as well as well as a couple of classical Greek references.

But the poem that has become known simply as *"Oran Eile"* (Another Song), plays no such games: in the third line, *"tha durrag air ghur ann am chail"* (a worm is broody in my being) he establishes the metaphor for his condition, dying of love and tuberculosis. An utterly moving poem, its effect on Sorley MacLean was potent, attracting his attention through poetry:

Uilleam Ros, de chanamaid
ag coinneachadh taobh thall a bhais?
Dheanainn luaidh air d'Oran Eile.

(William Ross, what would we say
meeting on the other side of death?
I would mention your Oran Eile.)

And in prose, Maclean observed, "The strange thing about it to me is that
such a perfection of self-conscious technique should accompany such poignancy
of emotion [...]." MacLean himself would achieve a similar marriage in many
poems, of which "*Coin is Madaidhean-allaidh*" (Dogs and Wolves) is a supreme
example. The poet himself said it came to him in the middle of the night, as if
from a dream.

If the poets discussed so far belong to the canon of Gaelic literature, as
defined by John MacKenzie, author of "*Sar-obair nam Bard Gaelach*", and
William J Watson author of "*Bardachd Ghaidhlig*" there were others, some
anonymous, some identifiable, who made important contributions to the
literature of Skye.

The recent collection of songs from Skye, "*Orain an Eilein*", edited by
Christine Martin, has done a great service in bringing together a wide range of
material, some of which I have already referred to. These include Mairi Nighean
Alasdair Ruadh, Lachlann Mac Thearlaich Oig and Uilleam Ros, all of whom
composed poetry that was intended to be sung. In that context, it is appropriate
to reflect that songs we have taken for granted, as songs, should also be counted
as poetry.

Among the many striking songs in "*Orain an Eilein*" "*Na Feidh am
Braigh Uige*" (The Deer in the Braes of Uig) is undated, and anonymous. With
its hunter lying on the moor, without coming home, this haunting song seems to
me to carry a distinct echo of the Border Ballad, "Twa Corbies". Many of the
other anonymous songs seem accidentally so: the subject matter is so specific, a
dignitary mourned or a lover celebrated or a lover betrayed.

Although we know that Beathag Mhor composed "*B'e siud an cul
bachallach*" (That was the curly head of hair) not much is known about her
personal life, other than the fact that she was from Duntulm and had a
relationship with Martainn a Bhealaich, with whom she had a child. She is
thought to have lived during the latter seventeenth and early eighteenth centuries
and was a dairymaid to the Martin family. However, she was not deemed good
enough for their son to marry. Her own child was taken into the custody of his
father's family, and she was obliged to observe her beloved bringing a bride
home from across the Minch. Out of the resultant anguish came the small corpus

of songs that survive. Beyond the vibrant directness of her language, and her craft, the quality that comes across most is an unusual generosity of spirit.

Tormod MacNeacail, (Norman Nicolson) son of the Clann Neacail of Sgoirebreac, was born at the end of the eighteenth century so his work really belongs to the nineteenth century. He is particularly remembered for one song, "*S gann gun dirich mi chaoidh*", lamenting the fact that he had been banned from the deer-forest on the instructions of his uncle, who happened to be a factor for Lord MacDonald. Tormod was to eventually die in Australia, having migrated there via Canada.

There is also a suggestion that Anna NicGilleathain from Sleat composed her song of unrequited love, "*Tha mi fo churam 's na ho ro eile*", for Tormad MacNeacail. She addresses her beloved as "Tormod" and there is a reference to her willingness to follow him across the ocean. However, like the relationship between Beathag Mhor and Martainn a Bhealaich, class and parental hostility blighted the relationship between Anna and Tormod.

Donald MacLeod, who had connections with the MacLeods of Raasay, is known to modern Gaels as Domhnall nan Oran, father of the more acclaimed Iain Dubh. John MacKenzie's book "*Sar-obair nam Bard Gaelach*" includes two poems by "*Am Bard Sgiathanach*" (The Skye Bard) who is identifiable as Domhnall nan Oran. Domhnall saw himself as occupying the role of Bard to the Clan MacLeod, and the two poems MacKenzie included had themes that reflected this aspiration. The poet's reputation now tends to rest on his satire on the "Black Elders of Lonmore" (*Eildearan Dubh a Loin Mhoir*) who refused to baptise his children.

Given that one of his sons, *Iain Dubh Dhomhnaill nan Oran* (Black John, son of Donald of the Songs) is said to have had knowledge of the black arts, maybe the elders knew more than they let on! Of Donald's two literary sons, Niall, who went to Edinburgh and was employed in the tea trade, was by far the more popular in his own time and for much of the twentieth century.

There is something of the florid about Niall's poetry, a sense of "putting on the style". There is no lack of technique or feeling for the language since his eloquence is undoubted and unforced. Unfortunately, the real spark that ignites the imagination of any reader is often missing. His praise poem for the island, while attractive, is essentially decorative rather than profound. There is also the question whether some of the songs attributed to him in his collection, like "*Clarsach an Doire*" should not actually belong in the Iain Dubh canon.

Iain Dubh, on the other hand, had no such pretensions. He was a merchant seaman, whose alleged knowledge of "the black arts" sounds suspiciously like the hypnosis and sleight of hand he may have acquired from a stage magician. Iain composed songs that addressed their themes with a refreshing directness. The pleasures and anguishes of the mariner's life are dealt with both poignantly and with sharp wit as appropriate, in language that gives the impression of being built on conversational speech patterns, while the rhythms and rhyme schemes are evidence of his craftsmanship.

The Macleod brothers could be regarded as economic exiles since they were perhaps less touched than others by the great upheavals affecting their homeland. Niall, however, does address the Clearances in his composition "*Muinntir a Ghlinne Seo*" (People of this Glen).

It was another Skye poet who, though also living in exile, gave persuasive voice to the people under threat, and to their predicament. A reference in one of the songs of *Mairi Mhor nan Oran* (Great Mary of the Songs) indicates she was provoked into verse on being imprisoned after having been falsely accused of theft. Whatever the cause, it released a muse in Mary MacPherson (née MacDonald) that would speak, with passion and eloquence, for her native island and its suffering people.

Mairi Mhor was not an innovator, in language or technique. Her techniques were tried and tested, the language she had in abundance. Mairi Mhor was also not a political sophisticate. She blamed the "*Sasunnaich*" for rack-renting and clearing her people, though the guilty parties were to be found much closer to home among the land-owning classes.

What Mairi Mhor brought to her poetry was a passionate commitment to the island and its people, and an unquenchable *joie de vivre*. That her songs inspired those who heard them is clear from accounts of her presence on public platforms, including the first National Mod, where she won a standing ovation, but no prizes. She rubbed shoulders with, and addressed poems to, members of the Land Law Reform movement leadership, like Charles Fraser MacIntosh. She also celebrated New Year's Day shinty matches between the Gaels of Glasgow. This may be why she composed songs like "*Nuair Bha Mi Og*" (When I was Young), which, for all that it could have become bogged down in nostalgia, comes across as a celebration of life, nature and survival. "*Eilean a' Cheo*" (Island of Mist) could be read as Mairi Mhor's Battle Hymn, and the "Song of Beinn Li" her victory song.

She may, with some justice, be regarded as the Laureate of the Highland Land League, but there was more to her than just that. Mairi Mhor's songs have become an essential part of the repertoire of Gaelic singers, not only because of their fine melodies but because her fine words still resonate with life and relevance. Her status as a poet, separate from the music also remains significant: her influence on the poets of the twentieth century is marked. More importantly, many of Mairi Mhor's songs remained in the memory of the Skye tradition-bearers, many of whom were themselves bards.

Perhaps because of the development of recording facilities, we now have access to the works of a considerable number of song poets from the twentieth century, and even those of a few earlier nineteenth century practitioners like the soldier-poet Iain Mac Dhomhnaill Mhic Alasdair. His composition, *"Airigh Luachrach Uige"* (Uig's Rushy Sheiling) survives, though most of his songs have been lost.

My own recollections of the two traditional bards I knew, Angus Fletcher and the Skipper, is that they could as readily have performed a song of Mairi Mhor's as one of their own. In fact, there is every reason to assume that all their fellow bards would have been able to do likewise. Although Sorley MacLean was no singer (he described himself as a "singer manque") his enthusiasm for Mairi Mhor was such that I am sure he could have recited as much of her work as a singer might have sung.

We will return to Sorley presently, but the continuing strength of the song tradition through the century deserves attention, given that compulsory education since 1872 had guaranteed Gaels literacy in English, while placing their own culture firmly on the margin. Yet the tradition endured, It survived the demise of the ceilidh house, in which a community congregated for its cultural exchanges and in the works of writer/performers like Calum and Rory MacDonald, it may be said to survive still.

It is not so long since every community had its own bard. Some of them are still remembered, some are on record, many are lost. I remember an old neighbour recalling that, in Idrigil, the Uig township of less than 40 crofts to which I belong, three neighbouring houses were each home to a bard. While I have no idea whether Seonaidh Mor 'Ain Chaimbeul was one of these three bards, his brother, Uilleam 'Ain Chaimbeul, did compose verses. Unfortunately, Uilleam had become religious by the time I was old enough to have had any interest in his songs, so I never heard any of his work. Nevertheless, in later life, he would still chant a traditional and utterly local song like *"'S fhad bhuam fhin bonn Beinn*

Eadarra" (Far from me the foot of Ben Edra). I did hear Angus Fletcher, who lived across the bay, perform his own songs on more than one occasion, and the Skipper — Iain MacNeacail, a distant relative — on many occasions.

Domhnall 'Ain Shomhairle is someone whose name often arose in family conversations, as he was my father's first cousin (and apparently a bit of a character), so it was intriguing to find two of his love songs in Christine Martin's anthology. However, she did not include the song most people remember him by, which recalls how he pawned his father's gramaphone in order to buy drink. Domhnall 'Ain Shomhairle was a soldier, as was Seonaidh Mor 'Ain Chaimbeul, who saw action during the First World War. I also note a Niall MacNeacail, from Brogaig, who may also have been a relative of mine. He, like Seonaidh Mor 'Ain Chaimbeul, seems to have emigrated to Australia.

There are others, like Charles Matheson from Braes, known to most as Tearlach a Phost, and Staffin-born Neil Beaton, whose by-name was Neil Gow. Their works have tended to be known to, and highly regarded by, singers, but have remained, until the Martin book, firmly in the oral tradition. Perhaps the most interesting figure in that anthology is Catriona Douglas. She is responsible for one of the most popular (if also one of the least memorable) songs in the Gaelic repertoire, "Morag of Dunvegan". Christine Martin also credits Catriona Douglas with authorship of songs like "*Nochd gun chadal*" (Tonight without sleep) and "*Chaill mi mo chridhe 's mi og*" (I lost my heart while still young), both of which have the timeless quality of a classic folk song.

Only three of the twentieth century Skye song poets have had their work published in collected form. Some years ago the School of Scottish Studies produced an album of the songs of Calum Ruadh MacNeacail, from Braes, with a book from Gairm Publications. Although his titles indicate a certain bardic ambition, with poems addressing the sinking of the "Hood", the Battle of Arnhem, the Paris Peace Treaty and the Nuremberg Trials, among other public themes, the result is workmanlike rather than inspired. A song to Spring, on the other hand, offers no rhetorical flight of fancy, but stays rooted in the decidedly unsentimental reality of the dung heap, from which he must gather manure to fertilise his crops.

A small selection of Angus Fletcher's work was assembled in a shared publication with the Skipper and produced, with accompanying cassette, by Catriona Montgomery as a small pamphlet publication. Angus's reputation rests on his facility for humorous topical verse, although he also composed love poetry.

Fletcher's stable-mate in that venture, would later be the subject of an academic thesis by Tom McKean, published under the title, "Hebridean Songmaker: Iain MacNeacail of the Isle of Skye". Universally known as the "Skipper", although never a mariner, he once told me, "If I had known when I was young that people would ever take my poetry seriously, I'd have taken it more seriously myself." McKean assembled thirty out of the hundred poems he reckoned to have composed, and revealed a man of many moods, deep knowledge of his own tradition, and the same eloquent directness that characterised the poems of Iain Dubh Dhomhnaill nan Orain. Humorous verse, social comment, gentle satire and love poetry feature, but he will be best remembered, perhaps, for his song composed in the Normandy trenches during World War Two, "*Nochd gur luaineach mo chadal*" (Restless my sleep tonight).

The other Skye-man to leave a memorable poetic record of the same conflict was a different kind of poet altogether. If the Skipper represented the survival of an unbroken song tradition, Sorley MacLean, while immersed in that tradition, brought influences and qualities to Gaelic poetry that projected it into an orbit where it now stands among the great literatures of the world.

Sorley was not the first Gaelic writer of the twentieth century to have had a university education, nor was he the first to essay poetry. The Rev. Kenneth MacLeod, although born on the Isle of Eigg, was of Skye parentage. He attended Glasgow University, though ill-health prevented him taking a degree. Similarly, the Rev. Neil Ross was an Edinburgh University graduate, as was the Rev. Angus MacKinnon, who followed the example of Dugald Buchanan, in destroying all his secular verse. This is a great pity because his religious poetry has considerable subtlety and character. MacLeod was Marjorie Kennedy Fraser's collaborator, while Ross's attempt at an epic account of the Second World War, "Armageddon" which was curtailed by his death, is essentially reportage, crafted into stately quatrains infused with elements of biblical imagery.

While steeped in his own history to the extent that the young Sorley was reported to have wept for the MacLeans killed at the Battle of Inverkeithing, centuries before — as if it were an event of the previous day — MacLean's was a restless mind. Having studied French, Gaelic and Latin at school in Portree, he went on to study English and French at Edinburgh University. While there he became familiar with, and in the early stages of his career emulated, the poetry of Ezra Pond and T.S. Eliot, though he soon decided that the English language was not a suitable medium for his craft. He was also much taken with, and influenced by, the seventeenth century English metaphysical poets, and with the poetry of French and Russian symbolists like Baudelaire and Aleksandr Blok, as well as the giant of Anglo-Irish literature, William Butler Yeats.

But Sorley was first and foremost a man of his time, and place. He grew up in the presence of people who had been physically cleared from their land, and who had campaigned for their rights to security of tenure on the land they still occupied. His own uncle was one of the first witnesses to appear in front of the Napier Commission. At a young age, Sorley rejected religion, though discreetly, since he had no wish to cause his parents offence. In later years he observed from more than one public platform that he had been "born into the Free Presbyterian Church; a small sect that consigns all the rest of humanity, and the great majority of its own adherents, to eternal hell-fire and damnation." He also adopted socialism as a personal philosophy that underwrote his life and much of his work, without ever reducing the poetry to mere polemic, even in such overtly political poems as *"Bana Ghaidheal"* (A Highland Woman) and *"Calbharaidh"* (Calvary).

Given his own chronological proximity to her time, and sympathy with the cause she represented, it is hardly surprising that Sorley regarded Mairi Mhor nan Oran as a significant influence on his work. Using both his awareness of the crofter's struggle, and Mairi Mhor's place in it, to bear on the convoluted politics of the time as Fascism spread across Europe, for the urban poverty Sorley observed in *"Calbharaidh"*, and its rural equivalent in *"Bana Ghaidheal"*, Mairi Mhor was an appropriate model.

He had other Gaelic models, of course: he was particularly drawn to the old, usually anonymous, songs that seemed to speak from their creators' being. Though no singer himself, Sorley sought to make his words sing for him. Indeed, the distinguished composer Ronald Stevenson who was a friend of Sorley's, and who set a number of his poems to music, has remarked that Sorley's work is difficult to set to music, because there is so much music in the words already.

The unrequited love that Uilleam Ros had for Marion Ross (like that of Yeats for Maud Gonne) struck a particular chord with MacLean, whose own blighted love-life in the 1930s provided the core theme for *"Dain do Eimhir"*. Here, his troubled relationships with two women are interwoven with the politics of the Spanish Civil War, filial duties, elements of Celtic mythology, European history, and an extraordinary visionary quality. This latter element crystallises in poems like *"Coin is Madaidhean Allaidh"* (Dogs and Wolves) which Sorley claimed came to him entire, in the middle of the night, as if he had dreamed it.

Once he had completed the set of poems centred on that Eimhir sequence (which included the long poem *"Coilltean Ratharsair"* (The Woods of Raasay), MacLean's output was relatively slow. Five short poems set him, along with fellow Gael George Campbell Hay, among the major war poets of 1939-45. Sections from the long poem *"An Cuilthionn"*, parts of which he had reservations about, eventually appeared in print, as did his unfinished meditation on "The Cave of Gold". Others which have appeared in print include the astonishing *"Hallaig"*, which populates the mind of the reader, as well as the eponymous deserted village, with slender birch trees become young women, striding out in the "dumb living twilight" of the evening.

There must have been times when the poet thought he was in the "dumb living twilight" of his culture. In one poem, he spoke *of "cur smuainteann an cainnt bhasmhor"* (putting thoughts in a dying tongue). But, whatever the statistics say, the reality, particularly in literary terms, has been very different. Sorley MacLean's achievement has provoked a flowering of Gaelic poetry in the twentieth century that, arguably, at least equals the eighteenth. All the Scottish Gaelic poets who came after him have, at one time or another, acknowledged his influence, including those who were, relatively speaking, his contemporaries.

For the next generation, including myself, Maoilios Caimbeul and the Montgomery sisters, all of us from Skye, Sorley was our literary Cuillin, the peak of twentieth century poetry, taking his place in the ridge of excellence alongside Mairi Mhor, Uilleam Ros and Mairi Nighean Alasdair Ruaidh. Of course, his very greatness could have been an inhibiting factor, but our existence is a demonstration that he has had the opposite effect. Sorley's openness to other influences, his references to Blok, and the English poet Cornford who was killed in Spain, among others, has encouraged us to follow our own curiosity into diverse alternative fields of influence.

For example, Maolios Caimbeul (a considerable poet, who should be much better known than he is) has pitted his Presbyterian background against a preoccupation with Confucianism. I have explored aspects of zen, as well as the European concision of poets like Miroslav Holub and the tumultuous Latin sensuousness of Pablo Neruda. Catriona Montgomery (who shares MacLean's lyrical gift) has translated Gerald Manley Hopkins. Morag Montgomery (who, by the way, has not published nearly enough), studied art and shows distinct traces of surrealism. We have all been open to the 'poetries' of many cultures, each without losing sight of the sound qualities and rhythmic currents of our own.

And now that time has placed us in a position of seniority, we can look to a further stream of writers making poetry in, and from, Skye, and in Gaelic. Among the youngest, Aonghas MacLeoid is a native of Skye. Angus Peter Campbell is a native speaker, originally from South Uist, and schooled under the influence of Iain Crichton Smith in Oban. Angus writes poetry and prose in both Gaelic and English. Iain Mac a Phearsain, of Skye and Islay descent, returned from Canada to reclaim his cultural heritage at Sabhal Mor Ostaig, where the present Writer in Residence is an Argyllshire-man, Rob Mac Illechiar, who also came to the college to improve his Gaelic.

In some ways the most improbable Gaelic poets in this most recent wave are already the best known. Meg Bateman (whose poetry is marked by subtle delicacy and candour), also began her journey to Gaelic fluency at Sabhal Mor, having been born and brought up in Edinburgh by English parents. Given her detailed study of the classical poets, it should perhaps be no cause for wonder that she has a facility for compositions that use classical techniques to great effect. Rody Gorman is a Dubliner by birth, and has lately come round to writing in the Irish Gaelic he grew up with, having gained a deserved reputation for his pithy poems in Scottish Gaelic.

All in all, the story of poetry in Skye is a continuing one. My list should not be regarded as inclusive. There are other poets (I suspect both older and younger) making poems according to both old and new rules. What is happening in Skye, and what I have sought to present a historical sketch of here, can be regarded as a microcosm. This ranges from classical bards and song poets, using tried and tested forms, to experimentalists and explorers. It ranges from original genius to the everyday practitioner. In every century, Skye has provided its share. Judging from the available evidence, the well is not about to run dry.

References

Black, Ronald (2001) *An Lasair*: Anthology of 18th Century Scottish Gaelic Verse. Edinburgh.
Black, Ronald (1999) *An Tuil*: Anthology of 20th Century Scottish Gaelic Verse. Edinburgh.
Mackenzie, John (1841) *Sar-obair nan Bard Gaelach* or *The Beauties of Gaelic Poetry*. Edinburgh.

Nicolson, Alexander (2nd ed. 1994) *History of Skye: a record of the families, the social conditions and the literature of the island*. Portree.

MacLeod, Fred T. (1917) *Eilean a'Cheo*, The Isle of Mist. Edinburgh.

Mhartainn, Cairistiona (2001) *Orain an Eilein*. An t-Eilean Sgitheanach.

Lamont, Rev. D.M. (1913) *Strath In Isle of Skye*. Glasgow.

Thomson, Derick (1983) *The Companion to Gaelic Scotland*. Oxford.

Thomson, Derick (2nd ed. 1990) *Introduction to Gaelic Poetry*. Edinburgh.

Royle, Trevor (1993) *The Mainstream Companion to Scottish Literature*. Edinburgh.

Watson, Roderick (1984) *The Literature of Scotland*. Basingstoke.

Watson, William J. (1932) *Bardachd Ghaidhlig* Specimens of Gaelic Poetry 1550-1900. Stirling.

Scottish Society for Northern Studies Publications